Count Your Blessings

Sandy Ludwig

Ludwig/New Harbor Press
1601 Mt. Rushmore Rd, Ste 3288
Rapid City, SD 57701
www.NewHarborPress.com

Count Your Blessings/Sandy Ludwig —1st ed.
ISBN 978-1-63357-358-1

All the references to child abuse cases are based on actual situations. Names have been changed to protect the individuals involved.

Contents

CHAPTER 1

A Call for Help

MADISON ROPER – A.K.A Maddie or Mads Roper – was dressed in a witch's costume with a black cape, a black face, a wart on her nose, and a tall black hat. She stood in the open doorway of St. Peter's Congregational United Church of Christ's social hall and grinned at all the children in their Halloween costumes. She counted nearly twenty-five kids in all, ranging in ages from one year to eighteen. She nearly giggled at some of their costumes, which included angels and devils, Star Wars robots and cute little kittens. She watched as her charges laughed and played, full of excitement and expectation. Their parents sat along the walls with their cups of decaf coffee and cookies. Everyone was waiting for the festivities to begin. Games, races, and awards for costumes were planned.

Maddie was just about to yell to get everyone's attention when the phone rang. She hurried over to it and snatched it up, moving outside into the hall so she could hear better.

"This is Mimi Durant," sobbed the lady on the line. Maddie recognized her immediately as a member of the church and automatically pictured a thin, shy woman with a tentative smile who never seemed very sure of herself.

"What's wrong, Mimi?"

"It's Fred! He's hitting Dawn for coming home late from school and right now he's pushing her out the door! I'm afraid of what he'll do next!"

"What's your address, Mimi? . . .Okay, thanks! I'm on my way!" Maddie hung up the phone, spotted Joan Perez, her assistant with the Halloween party, and hurried over to her.

"Take over, Joan. I've got an emergency. And when my dad comes in, please tell him I'm over at the Durant house, possibly dealing with child abuse. See you later!" Joan stared after her, mouth agape, then snapped out of it and got ready to take over the party.

Maddie, her cape flying behind her and holding on tight to her hat so the brisk Colorado wind wouldn't yank it off her head, rushed out to her car. She was a caseworker with Child Protective Services, part of the Department of Children, Youth and Families. Mimi Durant called her because she knew that.

Driving quickly over there, Maddie worried about what was going on and how to handle it. The situation sounded serious and she regretted being in her witch's costume. She wasn't sure Mr. Durant, a stern man who held himself rigidly all the time and seemed to look down on others, especially women, would take her seriously looking the way she did. Turning the corner onto their street, she prayed for guidance to do and say the right things, then pulled into their driveway and stopped behind the Durant car. Fred Durant stood at the front of his car on his steeply slanted driveway, yelling down at Dawn who huddled at the rear of the car, keeping it between her and her father. Mimi stood halfway between them, begging her husband to calm down. She saw Maddie approach and relief showed on her face.

Getting out of her car, Maddie's heart was racing. There was nothing she could do about looking like a silly witch, so she took a calming breath and slowly approached the family. She stopped by Dawn and found herself looking way up at Durant, a tall, imposing man even on level ground, while she, even in her shoes, was barely 5"3'. Despite that, she knew she had to take charge of this situation for Dawn's sake.

"Mr. Durant. I'm Madison Roper from church. I'm also a Child Protective Services caseworker and I'm here because I was called. Can we go inside and talk about what's going on?"

Durant turned his smoldering gaze from Dawn onto Maddie and just stared at her. Finally, he blinked and said, "You're the pastor's daughter, right?"

"Yes, I am. But I'm here as a CPS worker tonight to help you resolve this problem. If you'll let me."

Durant looked her over, from silly hat to blackened face to the rest of the costume. He scoffed. "I doubt it," he sneered, his lips turning down.

Lowering her voice, she said, "Mr. Durant, many of your neighbors are staring out their windows right now, watching you and wondering if they should call the police before you hurt Dawn. It might be wise if we go inside and talk. What do you say?" Maddie did her best to be non-threatening and pleasant, communicating confidence that they could settle the problem.

"I don't want her in my house! She stays out here!" he replied firmly, pointing at Dawn.

Mimi moved a little toward her husband. "Fred, it's too cold out here and Dawn doesn't even have a sweater on. Please, let's all go inside. Please!"

No reply.

"Fred, I'm begging you," pleaded Mimi, "we're all freezing out here, even you. Let's go inside," and she reached out to touch her husband's arm, but he shrugged her off. Maddie had stopped by Dawn and offered her hand to the girl. Dawn grasped it tightly, shaking with cold and nervousness. Together they started walking toward Dawn's mother. When they were together, Maddie took a hold of Mimi's hand too and the three of them headed for the front door. Durant stood rock still, blocking their way so they carefully veered around him and continued on. At the door, Maddie stopped and turned back.

"Mr. Durant, I want to hear your side of the story and find out what you're so angry about. Could you please come into the house so we can talk? Maybe together we can come up with a solution to the problem. Please." Maddie waited for him to turn around, which he finally did, and motioned for him to enter the house before her. He did so with a heavy sigh of resignation. Inside, he commandeered the couch and left the easy chairs for the women. He continued to glare at Dawn, who refused to look back at him, keeping her eyes lowered. Mimi grabbed an afghan and wrapped it around Dawn's shoulders.

Maddie waited for them to get settled, then turned to Durant. "Tell me what happened, sir," she said, giving him her complete attention, even sitting forward in her chair to show her good faith. She didn't know Durant very well; he seldom came to church with Mimi and Dawn. But she wanted to treat him with the same fairness as she treated all her clients. She nodded for him to begin.

After letting out another sigh, he stated angrily, "She dared to come home two hours late from school and lie to me about where she'd been! I know she lied to me because I called all her girlfriends and no one had seen her since school let out, yet she said she was with one of those girls! Then I smelled alcohol on her breath, a forbidden substance in this house and she knows it!"

Maddie nodded to let him know she understood how he could be angry about Dawn's tardiness, lies, and consuming alcohol. She gave him a moment to calm himself down.

"Then what did you do?"

"Frankly, I slapped her and I'm not ashamed of it!"

"That's not all you did, Fred," Mimi said. She was standing behind Dawn's chair, rubbing Dawn's shoulders to get her warmed up. "You slapped her repeatedly – look Maddie, you can see the bruise marks on her cheeks! Then you knocked her down to the floor and kicked her. You kicked her! Then you dragged her up by her hair and pushed her outside into the cold!"

Fred stared stonily at his wife and said nothing.

After a long moment of silence, Maddie asked, "Is that true, Mr. Durant?" All three stared at him waiting for his answer. Maddie thought she saw a brief flicker of emotion behind his eyes but it was fleeting and gone before she could be sure.

"Mr. Durant? Is what Mimi said true?"

"Yes! Dammit, it is! I have a right to discipline my own child the way I want to, don't I?"

"Actually, no, sir. Not when it leaves bruises or poses a danger to the child. Slapping, kicking, pushing her out into freezing weather – those are considered child abuse by the authorities." Maddie waited for him to digest that and make a comment, but he said nothing.

In the silence that followed, Maddie turned to face Dawn. "Dawn, I'd like to hear your side of the story now, please." Dawn hesitated, looking fearfully at her father. Mimi hugged her to give her courage. "Dawn, your father isn't going to do anything to hurt you again. It's safe for you to tell me why you were late and smelled of alcohol," said Maddie, giving her the most reassuring smile she could under all her witch's makeup.

She looked briefly at Fred Durant for his acknowledgement. He finally nodded okay.

Reassured, Dawn snuggled down into the afghan and explained in an unsteady voice, "When I left school, my old boyfriend swung by and offered me a ride home. I didn't really want to go with him but it was really cold out and so I agreed. But he didn't bring me home," she said, tearing up. "He drove up into the mountains towards Pike's Peak, and off into a campground where several trailers were parked. I kept telling him I wanted to go home but he grabbed a hold of my jacket and pulled me into one of the trailers. Then he brought out a bottle of alcohol from his backpack and started drinking. He offered the bottle to me. I took a swallow because I was freezing and scared. Then I took a second swallow for courage because I knew he was going to force me to have sex with him. When he did, I tried to fight him, I really did, Dad! But he was too strong! He raped me, then laughing and drunk he brought me home and dropped me off. I knew I was in trouble, so I lied about where I was. I was afraid of what you would do to me, Dad." Dawn burst into fresh tears at the memory. Mimi hugged her tightly, tears shining in her eyes as well.

Eyes flashing, Durant started to say something, but Maddie held up her hand to stop him. "Is there anything else I need to know, Dawn?"

"I didn't go with him to have sex with him! Please believe me! I really thought he would drive me home. Please believe me, Dad!" She stared straight at her father, imploring him with her eyes to believe her. "I couldn't stop him! He forced me!" She wept some more. Mimi got some tissues for her and cradled her.

"Which old boyfriend was it?" demanded Durant.

"No, Dad, it doesn't matter."

"Tell me!" He was breathing hard.

"Ollie Oleson."

"Why the hell did you ever get in his car?" he exploded.

"I was cold!"

Durant rose swiftly from the couch, a threatening look in his eyes. "I'll kill him!"

Maddie stood up quickly and reached a hand toward his arm. "Mr. Durant, please don't make such a threat! The police will take that very seriously if anything should happen to Ollie."

"Get her out of here! I can't stand looking at her anymore! I'm sorry she got raped but it was her own damn fault for getting into that jerk's car!"

"Sit down, Mr. Durant!" ordered Maddie firmly. She waited him out until, exasperated, he sat. "This is what I propose, sir.

I'm going to have Mimi put some clothes together in a bag for Dawn and I'm going to take her to our emergency shelter. I will also have her seen by a doctor and have a rape kit done. Do not, I repeat, do not do anything to Ollie! Do you understand?" She stood directly in front of him waiting for his answer. He looked at her for a long minute defiantly, but at last his rigid shoulders slumped and he nodded.

"Get her clothes, Mimi," he ordered. "And you," he said to Maddie, "get her out of here!"

CHAPTER 2

Maddie

"WELL, GOOD MORNING, MADS," greeted Gary Roper, her father, as she came through the kitchen doorway. He was sitting at the kitchen table eating cereal and drinking coffee.

"Coffee, I need coffee," she said, heading straight over to the pot to pour herself a cup. She didn't usually stop for coffee in the mornings, but she was going into work late because of the late-night she'd had with the Durants and needed something to wake her up. Getting Dawn settled in the shelter, taking her to the hospital to be checked over and a rape kit done, talking with the police and making a report on Ollie Oleson, the nineteen-year old who forced sex on Dawn, who is only sixteen, and finally making a call to Janie Cosgrove, her supervisor at CPS, to report the incident and start a case file on the Durant family. They would find a foster home for Dawn in a day or two and set a court hearing for the parents.

"I hear you had a busy night last night," commented Roper, half grinning, half serious. He was a ruddy-complexioned man of average height, wore glasses, and always had a twinkle in his eye as if something funny was about to happen any minute. He looked lovingly at Maddie, whom he thought of as his spitfire daughter.

"I missed the Halloween party. Did Joan tell you about the Durant call?"

"Yes. What's going on?"

"Fred went off the deep end because Dawn came home late from school, smelling of alcohol, and lied about where she'd been. Granted, those were all things for a parent to be upset about, but that man didn't even give Dawn a chance to explain why or what happened. He just reacted and became abusive toward her. Mimi called me at church. I went right out to their house, heard their stories, and took Dawn to the emergency shelter. That family will need a lot of work, but I may or may not be the one assigned to the case since I know the family."

Roper studied his daughter, her red hair, blue-green eyes, freckles everywhere. She had a heart of gold, an abundance of compassion for hurting people, and the ability to advocate for abused children. It was her nature to take them under her wing and provide the nurturing that they lacked. She was a jewel of a person, good to the core, and he was very proud of her. He found Maddie attractive, although maybe not beautiful in the classic sense. And maybe she was a little too intense sometimes. Yup, he thought to himself, she had all her mother's qualities and he smiled. How dearly he loved both of his girls!

The only sour spot was Maddie's divorce, he mused. Her ex-husband, Joe Skeeter, had initially come across as a victim when she first met him so, naturally, her heart went out to him. He was a charming guy back then with a boyish grin, but he was so needy for affection and praise. Roper could see that right away, but not Maddie. After they married, Roper watched with grave misgivings as Joe gradually changed, dropping the charm, and starting to drink. That cost him his job. Then he started finding fault with every little thing Maddie did, until the marriage – what was left of it – had degenerated into daily arguments and fights. The first time Joe hit her, though, it was like her eyes opened to the truth about him. The second time he beat her up badly, causing her to lose her baby. She started the divorce process immediately and moved out of their apartment. She came home to them – temporarily, of course. Eighteen months later she was still here. Roper chuckled. Fortunately, he thought, there were no other children to get caught in the crosshairs. Yet he dreamed of Madison finding a man who would love her and treat her like the princess that she was. Hmm, he thought, there was one new member in the church, early thirties, single, who seemed pleasant enough, name of Rick Shelby. A possibility? Maybe. . .

Maddie sat at the table with her father and finished her coffee. "You might want to talk with Fred Durant, Dad. I've never seen him so worked up, so unyielding as he was last night. Maybe he'd open up with you and you could counsel him."

"If he'd be willing. I can't force him, you know."

"I know. The judge will probably order him go to anger control and parenting classes. It was just a thought I had. He needs a friend right now."

Smiling, Roper nodded. "If he wants me to be there for him, I will."

"Great! Time for me to get to work or I'll get chewed out."

"I doubt that. I'm sure your supervisor, Janie Cosgrove, encouraged you to sleep in this morning since you were up half the night, right?"

Grinning, Maddie rose and went over and kissed her father on the forehead, then took her cup to the sink. "Janie told me to take the whole morning off. An investigator will talk to everyone in the family and finish making the report. But if Dawn goes into foster care, I hope it becomes my case. I'd like to work with the family. Gotta go, Dad. See you later!"

Maddie was humming to herself as she drove to the Child Protective Services office building. She, like most of her coworkers, simply referred to it as CPS. She went in search of Janie when she arrived. Janie was an elegant, light-colored black lady married to a retired Army vet whom she always referred to by his last name or even just Cos. A habit, she explained, left over from military life. Janie had the charming ability to talk people into doing things the way she liked. She gently wielded her power over administration as well as other supervisors and her caseworkers. Everyone adored Janie and gladly did her bidding. Maddie was sure Janie would be head of administration one of these days.

"Good morning, Janie," she greeted her, standing in her doorway.

After checking her watch, Janie smiled and said, "Yes, by golly, it is still morning, and a good one at that. But you weren't supposed to be in until this afternoon—not that I really expected you to follow my suggestion. Anyway, have a seat and tell me about your night last night."

Maddie sat down and related the whole scenario with the Durants word for word. "Understand that I was in a witch's costume for a Halloween party for the kids at our church when I got the call. I felt silly and unprofessional, but there was no time to go home and change."

Janie chuckled, picturing it. "Dawn's at the emergency shelter now?"

"Yes, until she gets placed with a foster family or goes back home."

"Sounds like you feel the father is too belligerent to leave Dawn at home and make this an In-home case. How about if we throw in some anger control and parenting classes? Do you think that would suffice?"

Maddie shook her head. "If you'd seen the rage in that man's eyes you wouldn't suggest that. He definitely needs those classes, but he also needs time away from Dawn to cool off."

"And his wife? How does she fit in here?"

"Mimi is not strong enough to control her husband. She was crying and pleading with him but kept her distance from him."

"Why did she call you at the church?"

"Because she knew I'd be there for the Halloween party, which Dawn was supposed to attend."

"So, she knows you work for CPS." Maddie nodded. "Okay, let me find out what Intake has found out. I'll get back to you in a little bit. Good work, Maddie!" Janie gave her a big smile and was about to dismiss her when she thought of something. "By the way, we just hired a new caseworker who will probably shadow the worker on the Durant case. We'll have a powwow with the two of them as soon as I can set it up."

"Thanks, Janie."

Maddie let out a breath and headed for her office. Inside she flipped on the light and dropped her purse and briefcase on the desk, then sat. Immediately, Marcia Peabody, the foster care team's secretary, popped her head in.

"A lady called for you this morning, named—" she looked down at the message slip in her hand—"Mimi Durant. She wants you to call her back right away. Here's her number."

Maddie took the piece of paper from Marcia and dialed the number right away. She figured Mimi had a bunch of questions for her, but it was too soon to have any answers yet.

"Maddie? Thank you for calling back." Mimi was crying again. "I'm worried about Fred. He left last night after you and Dawn left, and he hasn't returned yet this morning! I have no idea where he is. He was so distraught last night; I'm scared he'll do something terrible!"

"You mean like hurt himself?"

"I don't know!" she cried. "He's never done anything like this before! Please, find him, Maddie."

"I'll have the assigned caseworker file a missing person's report and explain the situation to the police. Since this is now an open CPS case, the police should get right on it. But, Mimi, if and when he comes home, give us a call right away, okay?"

"Yes, I will." Maddie hung up the phone worrying about the adult Durants as well as Dawn.

Janie called later to tell Maddie the meeting with the Intake investigator would be in ten minutes in the small conference room. Maddie picked up a pad and pen and her notes from the incident last night and headed over there. She was the first to arrive. Janie came in a few minutes later and then the investigator who turned out to be Jaime Gomez, one of her favorite people. The new fellow came also. He was introduced as Rick Shelby and Maddie did a double take. She recognized him. She'd seen him at church once or twice, although she didn't know his name. He was nice looking, even handsome, she thought, a strong athletic type guy with dark wavy hair, dark eyes, and dimples when he smiled. He looked at her and recognition dawned on him, too.

"Okay, let's get started," said Janie.

"Before we do," interrupted Maddie, "I need to mention that Fred Durant went missing last night. His wife just called me this morning to tell me. She's worried about him, said he's never done anything like this before."

"We'll alert the police," said Jaime. "When we're done here, I'll call Mrs. Durant and get a description of the man and his car's license number. But first, let's talk about Dawn. The doctor found bruises on her face and stomach where her father hit and kicked her. They also got a sample of the boyfriend's semen and if he's in the system, the police will find him. He's a nineteen-year-old, so he'll be prosecuted as an adult. Dawn is scared to go back home because of her father, so we're recommending foster care for the time being. I'll get the paperwork started to get a court hearing set up as soon as possible."

"Will Dawn's mother be able to visit her?" asked Maddie. "They're very close and she sided with Dawn the whole time and intervened for her. But she wasn't able to control her husband."

"Sure, we can set that up," answered Jaime. "Probably tomorrow."

They continued to discuss the situation further until they were satisfied that they'd covered everything. Jaime would handle the visit and he'd have the mother bring more clothes for Dawn at that time.

Janie then turned to Maddie and said, "I'm not going to assign the case to you, Maddie, because you know the family from your church. I hope you won't be disappointed. I got the feeling this morning that you'd like to work with them."

"I would, but I understand and I'm fine with it. Who will be assigned, do you know yet?"

"I'm considering Monica Tubbs."

Maddie kept a smile on her face but inwardly she groaned. Monica was fresh out of college with her social work degree and was convinced she knew more than anyone else did. She also had a put-offish way about her, could be prickly, and was definitely sarcastic. Oh, well. Monica had to report to Janie who would keep her in line. Maddie stood up and the others followed suit. Rick paused, eyes on Maddie.

"Can I talk to you a minute?" he asked.

"Sure," she said. "Walk with me to my office? I have tons of work to do.

"Be glad to. Don't know if you remember me or not," Rick began. "I just recently joined your father's church and I've seen you around. I didn't realize you worked here at CPS."

"I remember seeing you, too, Rick, but I didn't know you worked for CPS either. Is this your first day?"

"No, I started a couple of days ago, but I was in training."

They reached Maddie's office and went in. She laid her pad and notes on the desk and dropped into her desk chair, motioning for Rick to have a seat at the same time. Nice-looking guy, she thought again. No doubt married.

"Got questions for me, Rick? How can I help you?"

"Oh, just general questions, like how long have you worked here and what keeps you going? So far, in the two days I've been here, I've met three burned-out workers, at least five cynical ones, and a number of supervisors who seem to be ready to quit."

"Sounds about right. I've been here four years now and worked for a private adoption agency for two before that. I'm not burned out because I can't stand to see children abused and that keeps me motivated to advocate for them. I also have a strong faith in God and believe this is what He wants me to be doing. It's my ministry, in a way."

Rick sat there a moment, studying her. That was a clearest statement he'd ever heard from a social worker, not just "I like to help people." He could tell this was a calling for her.

"What about you?" Maddie asked in return. "Why are you a social worker?"

"I had a stint in the Army as a rookie Lieutenant and had an occasion to send one of my boys to Army Community Services for help with his anger management issues and met the social worker there who worked with him. I was impressed with her work—in fact, I fell in love with her and married her. My plan was to get my master's degree in social work when I got out of the Army and for Betty and me to be a team." He paused then, a faraway look in his eyes and Maddie saw sadness and regret there.

"What happened?" she asked quietly.

Rick replied, "Nothing dramatic. She simply fell out of love with me, wanted more glamor and excitement in her life. Said she was tired of social work and was going to move to Hollywood and become an actress. Haven't seen her name in lights yet, but who knows? Anyway, we divorced. But she urged me to pursue my social work degree, so I went ahead and got it, and here I am. I just moved to town last month, joined your church, and applied for a job here. Kind of surprised to get called so quickly, but I'm not complaining."

"So, this is your first actual social work job?"

"Yeah. I'm glad there's training and that I'll be trailing one of the experienced workers around for a while, but any hints you can give me will be appreciated."

"The main advice I can give you is taking care of yourself physically and mentally. When you leave to go home at night, try to leave your work here and don't think about your cases or all the work you have yet to do. Also, keep a little distance between you and your clients because they can really suck you in."

"What kind of caseload do you carry?"

"Right now, I have over thirty kids to visit and shepherd around, arrange parent-child visits, monitor issues and progress, etc., and attend hearings."

"Ages?"

"I have toddlers to teenagers. Almost all in foster care but some have been returned home that I'm following for a while before closing the cases."

"Bet you're organized and always on top of things."

"Right," she grinned. "Look," she said, sobering a bit, "I really need to get some work done since I got in late this morning. So . . ."

"I can take a hint," said Rick standing and grinning. "Don't work too hard. Take your own advice, okay? See you later." He sauntered out of her office with a wave.

For moment, Maddie sat back in her chair. Nice guy, she thought, comfortable with himself. Definitely not needy like Joe. With a sigh to rid herself of where those thoughts would take her, she sat up straighter and prepared to type up her notes from last night with the Durants and then review her reports on her other on-going cases. There was a team meeting scheduled for later in the afternoon in which Janie would check in with them on their cases and discuss the more difficult ones, meaning those with uncooperative parents or rebellious teenagers usually. It's not all peaches-and-cream once kids got placed in foster care, Maddie had learned. Despite being abused by their parents, many of the kids preferred to be home, and many dealt with their past trauma by picking up their parents' bad habits and perpetuating them.

One family she had worked with had a mother who did heroin and a father who was a thief and used his children to watch out for the police for him while on stealing rampages. Unfortunately for him, he and the four children were caught. He went to prison and CPS placed the children in good foster homes, two in one, two in another, believing they were helping the children. But all four of the kids became difficult to handle and caused havoc in the foster homes. The oldest, a sixteen-year old at the time, began drinking. The second had to be placed in a therapeutic home for troubled teens. The third stuffed his ears with earbuds and tuned everyone out. And the youngest child, a little girl of nine, cried relentlessly for her mother. Maddie got the mother into rehab, set up substantial visits between her and the children, and prayed her heart out for the mother to fight her habit and win. But once out of rehab she went right back to her supplier and got high again. That case was not a successful one and it ate at Maddie. She had gotten close to the oldest boy and it broke her heart to see him deteriorate into addiction like his mother. When he turned eighteen and was released from the foster care system he promptly disappeared into Denver and was lost to her.

Maddie smiled sadly at the memory of that family. The little girl was still in foster care, but she was getting hardened and cynical at the tender age of eleven.

Snap out of it, Maddie, she told herself. You've got too much work to do to dwell on disappointing cases like that one. She vaguely remembered being eager and optimistic in the beginning of her career as a social worker. It was certainly pleasant with the private adoption agency. But then Joe had entered her life and wanted to move away from the Colorado Springs area. They had moved down to Pueblo and lived there for a little over a year until she realized she wasn't going to be able to save him from himself. Then the world turned upside down for her. She had been so excited the day she found out she was pregnant that she waited up for Joe to come home. But when he came home, he was drunk as a skunk and started ranting and raving at her over something, she couldn't even remember what. Then he backhanded her and pushed her down, kicking her in the stomach. She lay there crying, cowering, waiting for him to stop beating her and collapse on the couch like he usually did. When she was positive he was out cold, she got up as quiet as a mouse, already knowing that she would lose the baby. She didn't even pack a bag for herself and snuck out of the house. She drove straight back to Colorado Springs to the church parsonage where her parents lived. They heard her sneak in at 5:00 AM and met her, encircling her with their love, compassion, and tears. She lost her baby that morning.

That was eighteen months ago. Maybe, thought Maddie ruefully, it was time now to find an apartment and move out of her parents' home. However, she felt so loved and safe there it was tempting to just stay. Still, at twenty-eight years of age, it was time to cut the umbilical cord and deal with life on her own. She sighed at the thought. Not today, she thought. Too busy. She had three family visits to make, a court case to prepare for, as well as the team meeting. Snapping out of her revere, Maddie got energized. It was time to type up her report on the Durants and get some lunch. Then it would be time to get on with the rest of the day.

Just as she was ready to break for lunch, she heard Monica Tubbs enter Janie's office and close the door, already yelling about her disastrous visit with the Durants, thanks to Rick Shelby. Maddie listened intently.

CHAPTER 3

Rick

RICK HEADED BACK TO his office after visiting with Maddie. It looked barren to him, not homey or personalized like her office. Of course, it had a desk, computer, two chairs, a filing cabinet and a bookcase. But it had nothing of him in it. No degrees on the walls, no plants or pictures. He needed to make it homier somehow. He wasn't sure exactly how, not being big on things. He was kind of a minimalist since his wife left him and took everything with her.

Sitting down, he thought about Maddie. He had noticed her right away at church, especially with her red hair and those aqua-blue eyes. Like a real Irish lass. Her father was no Irishman, that was for sure, but as soon as Rick saw Mrs. Roper, another red head, he knew where Maddie's Irish looks came from. Maddie was definitely a striking woman; she certainly caught his eye. She was also well-liked by everyone at church and she seemed to have a passion for kids, since she oversaw the youth group, worked with the senior high Sunday school class, and worked for CPS. A friend of his at church called him early this morning to tell him she had been called out last night during the Halloween party to help the Durant family and that she'd had to remove the girl. The church grapevine was as fast as any grapevine he'd come in contact with.

He was thinking about that when Monica Tubbs, the caseworker he was assigned to shadow to learn how caseworkers worked, stuck her head in his door and asked if he was busy. Obviously, he wasn't.

"Hello, I'm Monica Tubbs," she announced, "the caseworker assigned to the Durant case." He took her in in one fell swoop. About 5'7", slender, blond hair, blue eyes, with a good figure, but when she smiled the edges of her mouth turned down. He felt her eyes sizing him up at the same time and deciding she could handle him with one hand tied behind her back

"Hello, Monica," he said. He motioned her in and pointed to the chair. But Monica was all business; she remained standing at the door.

"I'm ready to go out and talk to the Durants. You're coming with me," she said in a bossy way.

"Now?" asked Rick.

"That's what I said, Shelby. Now."

Rick bristled at being called by his last name but didn't let it show on his face. "The name is Rick," he told her quietly, "unless you want me to call you Tubbs." He stood up, letting his height add emphasis to his words.

"Sorry. Couldn't remember it," she responded, unfazed. "Let's go. I'll drive."

He followed her out of the building to her car and dutifully got in the passenger's side. She was not going to be fun to work with, he decided. Well, he'd have to make do until his probation was over and he could work on his own.

"You're awful quiet," commented Monica after a few minutes. "Don't you have questions for me about the case?"

"Not yet. I haven't met the Durants and except for the briefing this morning, I don't know enough to ask specific questions. I'll wait until after the visit."

"Suit yourself. We'll be there in about ten minutes. In the meantime, tell me about yourself. Where'd you work before? Are you married? Have kids? Why'd you become a social worker?"

Rick hesitated, not wanting to share anything personal with this woman. "Not much to tell, really," he said evasively. "Except that I went into social work because I wanted to give back to the community."

"Why? Were you in the system yourself as a kid?"

"No, nothing like that. I'm just tired of seeing poor people, black and brown people, abused children, the disenfranchised, the mentally ill, and street people getting shafted, so I opted to do my part to help out where I could."

"So you're an altruist." She made it sound like an insult and Rick bit his tongue to keep from saying something he'd later regret. He couldn't wait to get to the Durant house and get her attention off him. As they got out of her car, the front door of the house opened and Mimi Durant appeared. Her eyes were red and puffy from crying all night; tears still ran down her cheeks.

"Mrs. Durant, we're from Child Protective Services," said Monica briskly. "I'm Monica Tubbs and this is a new worker I brought along to learn how we do things. May we come in?"

"Yes, please. Have the police found Fred yet?" she asked anxiously, following them into the living room.

"No, not yet."

Rick was surprised at Monica's rudeness in not introducing him and her less-than-compassionate tone of voice with Mrs. Durant. He commented, "I'm sure they'll find him soon, ma'am. The police are already looking for him."

"Oh, thank you, Mr. –

"Shelby, but please call me Rick."

Monica, not liking Rick trying to take over, jumped in and got down to business. "Mrs. Durant, I want you know that Dawn is doing well at the emergency shelter and will be placed in a foster home in due time. She'll be receiving counseling for being raped and the doctors will follow her should she get pregnant."

Mimi nodded but asked, "When can I see her?"

"That'll probably be next week some time."

"Next week?!" cried Mimi. "Why can't I see her today? Or tomorrow?" Fresh tears spewed from her eyes. "My husband's gone! My daughter's gone! I'm here all alone!" she wailed and covered her face with her hands and sobbed loudly. Rick waited to see if Monica would go over to Mrs. Durant to comfort and reassure her, but she remained sitting stiffly on her chair, so he went over and sat down beside the distraught woman. He tentatively put his arm around her shoulders, not sure if he was out of bounds but he just felt he had to show some kindness to this hurting, scared woman. He noticed Monica's pursed lips turn down with disapproval but he didn't care. What was that old saying? Do what you want to do and ask for forgiveness afterward?

Mimi Durant leaned into Rick, appreciating his support.

"We'll do what we can to arrange a visit as soon as possible between you and Dawn," he whispered in her ear.

Suddenly, the front door slammed open. Everyone jumped, eyes immediately riveted on the living room doorway where Fred Durant appeared and stood rigid and still, staring at Rick who was still hugging Mimi. Slowly, Rick removed his arm from her shoulder and stood up.

"Mr. Durant—"

"Shut up! How dare you embrace my wife! Who the hell are you, anyway?" he demanded. "And, who are you?" he bellowed at Monica.

Monica stood up and faced him, unflinching and superior. "I'm Monica Tubbs from Child Protective Services. I assume you're Fred Durant?" She looked at him fearlessly. Rick saw the look in her eyes that this was another man she could control.

Without answering her, he turned to Rick. "And you?"

"Rick Shelby, also of Child Protective Services, sir." He waited to see what Durant would do next.

But before anything happened, Mimi stood up and went over to her husband. "Oh, Fred! You don't know how glad I am that you're back home! You scared the daylights out of me, leaving like that last night and not coming home all night. I was so afraid that something happen to you. I wish you had called!"

"Shut up, Mimi, you're babbling! I'm not even gone twenty-four hours and you're embracing another man! What kind of Christian wife are you?"

"Oh, Fred, we weren't embracing!" she exclaimed. "I was crying, and he was just trying to comfort me."

"Comfort you!" Durant sneered. Then turning to Rick, he said, "Where's Madison Roper, the pastor's daughter, the caseworker who came here last night?"

Monica spoke up before Rick could, which was fine by him because Durant addressing him would put him in an even more awkward position with Monica.

"Mr. Durant, Madison is off the case. She only responded to your wife's call to her. She wasn't officially assigned to your case. I am your official caseworker. Rick here is just tagging along to learn the ropes."

"I will deal with no one from Child Protective Services except Madison Roper! Period! Now, both of you, out!"

"Aren't you even going to ask about your daughter, Mr. Durant? After all, she was raped as well as abused," asked Monica coldly.

"That was her own fault," he retorted, "and until she accepts responsibility for her stupid actions, I don't want to hear about her or talk to her. When she's ready to apologize to me, I'll reconsider then."

"But, Fred," said Mimi meekly, "she did apologize, several times last night."

Fred took a threatening step toward her, but Rick quickly inserted himself between them. “Not a good idea, Mr. Durant. Back off, sir.” Rick was nowhere near as tall as Durant, but he was well built from working out in the gym and mountain climbing. Durant locked eyes with him.

“Get out of my house!” he spat.

“Only if I have your word you will not lay a hand on your wife.”

“I said get out!”

“Without your promise, Mr. Durant, your wife will leave with us for her own safety.”

“Fred, please!” pleaded Mimi. “This nice young man was not embracing me but trying to calm me down from crying so much over Dawn and you leaving. I’m sorry it looked that way to you. I need you to hold me, Fred. Please!” Tears again flowed as she implored her husband to relent. Finally, sighing, Durant stepped back.

“You can leave,” he told Rick sullenly. “I won’t hurt my wife.” Rick studied him until he was satisfied he was telling the truth. Checking with Mimi, he accepted her nod that everything would be alright.

“We will get a visit arranged for you and Dawn as soon as we can, Mrs. Durant. We’ll give you a call,” said Rick, deliberately not waiting for Monica to speak first. Mimi smiled her thanks and clasped his hand.

On the way out to Monica’s car, Rick prepared himself to be reamed up one side and down the other by Monica. But in the car she said nothing; she wouldn’t even look at him. Instead, she just started the car, pulled sharply from the curb, stared straight ahead, and drove back to CPS. Her lips were in a tight straight line and Rick could tell she was seething with indignation. He began to feel uneasy that he had offended her more seriously than he thought. But he was only doing what a decent person would do, wasn’t he?

Back at CPS, Monica marched ahead of him, never looking back, and headed straight for Janie's office, slamming the door behind her. Rick's heart dropped to his stomach. But, surprising him, a couple of nearby workers grinned up at him, and one gave him a thumb's up sign. A female worker approached and whispered, "You must have done something right for her to be so pissed at you. She thinks she's the queen bee around here," and she patted Rick on the shoulder.

Despite the support he'd received, Rick went into his office and brooded. Did he blow this job on his first real day of work? It had felt like he was doing the right thing at the Durants. Well, when Monica was done eviscerating him, Janie would be in to give him his walking papers. He just knew it. He sat and waited, unable to concentrate on anything else.

But instead of Janie showing up at his door, Maddie came in and closed the door behind her. She was trying hard not to grin as she sat down in his visitor's chair. He wasn't sure if she was grinning happily for him, or because he was about to get canned, though that didn't seem like her style. She was silent a long moment.

"Say something!" he finally said into the silence.

Her laughter erupted then and was delightful, almost musical to Rick's ears. "Oh, Rick, I'm sorry!" she said, covering her mouth. "I'm not laughing at you. I could hear Monica ranting and raving to Janie about how you 'took over' her interview with the Durant family and made her look like a fool. How you intervened 'inappropriately' and upset Mr. Durant. How he then addressed you as the official caseworker and not her. She was livid! She told Janie she doesn't want to work with you, ever! In fact, she suggested Janie fire you immediately!" Maddie was still laughing when she finished talking.

"Am I going to be fired?" he asked quietly, seriously.

"Not a chance, Rick! Janie knows Monica well enough—in fact she probably teamed you up with her on purpose because she's such a cold fish and you would provide some of the kindness and sensitivity that the Durant family needed right now. Especially Mimi, who's probably as much of a victim as Dawn."

Rick quietly let out a breath of relief.

"What did you do that was so 'inappropriate,' anyway?"

He shrugged. "Mrs. Durant was crying her heart out over Dawn being taken and then her husband disappearing. She looked so lost. So I went over and sat next to her and kind of hugged her. Just an arm around her shoulders. She seemed to appreciate it. It's just that Mr. Durant decided to come home at that very moment, and it got awkward. He became accusatory with his wife and approached her threateningly, so I got between them and made him promise he wouldn't hurt her or we'd take her away with us to a safe place. Durant hesitated but he finally gave me his word he wouldn't harm her. He then addressed me and not Monica as lead caseworker and when she told him she was the caseworker, he sneered at her and said he'd only work with you."

"Me?" Maddie's mouth dropped open. "Monica didn't mention that. Oh boy! Now I'll be in the doghouse with her, too."

A knock at the door interrupted their conversation. Rick called come in and Janie opened the door.

"May I talk to you a minute, Rick? Oh, hello, Maddie. Please stay, this concerns you too."

"Of course." Maddie stood so Janie could have the chair.

Rick stood up politely, his stomach in knots. He wasn't as sure about his future at CPS as Maddie seemed to be.

"Rick, I'm sure you know why I'm here." He nodded. "Don't look so worried," she said, smiling reassuringly. "You're not in any trouble. I heard Monica's side of the story and then I called the Durants and got their side. Mr. Durant made it clear to me that he would not work with Monica because of her, uh, attitude. His word was less kind than that. He said he would work with Madison, however, and that you were welcome to continue as her 'assistant,' his word. So, I'm going to make an exception to the rule here and allow Maddie to have the Durant case even though the family attends her church and she knows the mother and daughter pretty well. You will be her 'assistant.' Rick, I want you to know how impressed I am with you in showing Mrs. Durant much needed compassion and in dealing firmly with Mr. Durant. You showed excellent judgment and skill. I think you will make a fine addition to our team here. Thank you."

"Thank you, Mrs. Cosgrove," Rick said earnestly, the knots in his stomach starting to unravel.

"Please, call me Janie like everyone else does. Now, tell me, is this arrangement agreeable to the two of you?"

Both agreed that it was.

"Great, then that's settled. I thank you both for being so accommodating." Janie rose from the chair and added, "I'll get the Durant file to you, Maddie, after Monica writes up her notes. I'd like you to write a report on the visit, too, Rick. Then you and Maddie can get together to review it and draw up the permanency plan for the family, arrange parent-child visits, and so on. I think you two will work well together. Maddie here has a heart of gold and is one of my favorite workers."

"Janie?" said Rick as Janie stood up. "I belong to Maddie's church, too, well her father's church, and I know the Durants by sight. Is that going to be a problem?"

"Did they recognize you from church?"

"No, neither of them."

"Okay, then, I'm going to leave it as is, with Maddie as lead caseworker and you second in command. I'd also like you to go out with her on all her cases starting today and become familiar with them. You'll learn the ropes as you go along."

"Thank you."

After Janie and Maddie departed, Rick sat and reflected on this development. He was relieved not to be fired and glad he'd be working with Maddie, but he felt bad that he had alienated

Monica. He got the impression that she was tolerated in the agency but not really liked. Well, he'd avoid her as much as he could and try not to upset anyone else.

A few minutes later, he decided to find a nearby restaurant for lunch and was on his way out of the building when he spotted Maddie getting into her car. Shoot, he thought, he'd have liked to have lunch with her, but she was already starting her car as he approached his. Maybe he'd follow her to the restaurant and "accidently" bump into her there. Chuckling, he decided to do just that.

To his surprise, Maddie was waiting at the door of the restaurant for him when he arrived.

"Uh, you caught me following you, didn't you?" he asked, coloring.

Grinning, she took in his charming discomfort in stride and said, "Yup. Join me for lunch?"

"Just what I was going to ask you," he responded, and they entered the restaurant together and got a table. Their conversation ranged from Monica to Janie to the church to the Durants. He felt comfortable with Maddie and was very glad he'd been assigned to her.

That afternoon he went with her to her three home visits. The first was Dom and Eunice Harper. Rick sized Dom up as a "happy drunk" while Eunice clearly was determined to get her drinking under control and get her two sons back. Maddie was gentle but firm in talking with Eunice about someday maybe having to make a choice between Dom and her children. She had nodded sadly.

"I keep praying for him that he'll come around," said Eunice.

"Keep praying," encouraged Maddie. "I will too."

Then they went to the Watsons. Jim was a Captain in the Army who was used to demanding total obedience from the men under him. Unfortunately, he did the same thing at home, expecting total obedience from his wife, Phyllis, and his children,

Jim Junior and Kathy, only six and three years of age. Phyllis didn't mind; she loved the strong, physically demanding side of her husband but was blind to how it affected the children. They didn't understand, but they knew to be afraid of their father if he got mad. Maddie worried that Watson would never learn to separate his career responsibilities from the way he fathered his children.

The Floyd case involved a single mother, Marnie, who danced at night, leaving her little five-year old daughter, Daisy, alone. A neighbor, Ginny Carrillo, took it upon herself to listen for the child's cries at night and often watched her during the morning while Marnie slept. One night, Daisy woke up and cried for her mother. Ginny, unfortunately, was over at her sister's house to nurse her following an operation, so she wasn't there to take care of Daisy. The child, crying and sobbing, wandered out of the house in search of her mother and was found several blocks away by an elderly man out for a late night stroll with his dog. He called the police and CPS got involved. Daisy was now in foster care and Maddie visited Marnie to see how she was progressing on finding a daytime job.

Their visit with Marnie was less than satisfactory. She made excuse after excuse for not finding a day job. Maddie warned her that the longer she stalled, the longer it would be before Daisy came home.

"That's okay," Marnie replied nonchalantly. "I've got another kid on the way. You can keep Daisy."

Maddie became still. She studied Marnie, a petite, attractive brunet, who, as soon as she saw Rick, had turned on her sexy charm and began flirting with him.

"Are you telling me that you want to terminate your parental rights to Daisy?" asked Maddie unbelievingly.

"Yeah," she answered. "I can always make more babies."

"Oh, Marnie," said Maddie sadly. "How can you give up that precious child? She's beautiful. She loves you so much. She gets so excited when it's time for a visit with you."

Marnie wouldn't look at Maddie. She just shrugged.

"Think hard about this, Marnie. It's permanent when you have your rights terminated."

Out in the car, Maddie was sad-looking as she sat and jotted down her mileage and a brief note on the visit. Rick watched her intently.

"Are you okay?" he asked.

After exhaling, she replied, "I guess, but I've been rooting for her for so long, trying to get her to comply. I like her. But she's obviously got a different agenda for her life now, and Daisy's, than I do."

"Are you going to terminate her rights?"

"Oh, no! Not yet. I'll talk with her again and again before I seriously consider it, and I'll also bring it up in a team meeting with Janie and the others before I follow through."

Maddie started the car. Rick became thoughtful, thinking about the clients they'd visited so far, and how differently Maddie dealt with each one. Different, yes, but always considerate, polite, and on their side. He liked how she emphasized the positive in their progress, how she rooted for them and cheered them on. It occurred to him that he should be taking notes on these visits, to get the hang of it, for when he carried a caseload of his own.

Maddie drove to the courthouse next where Rick sat and listened to her testify on the Darlene and Casper Brown case. They were apparently doing quite well. In fact, the judge ordered the kids, Judy, Barbie, Stevie, and Mellie, to be returned to them and they were clearly as eager and happy to be going home as their parents were to receive them.

"We're going to order a big pepperoni pizza for the occasion!" Casper was exclaiming to his family. Maddie smiled and shook their hands, congratulating them. The children hurried over to hug her and thank her.

"Will you still come see us, Maddie?"

"You betcha !" she told them and gave them each a tight hug. A happy ending. Ahh, she smiled to herself. They were few and far between, so she cherished each one. It kept her going. Checking her watch, Maddie saw they were already too late for the team meeting.

"Well," she said to Rick as they exited the courthouse, "I better call Janie and explain why we missed the team meeting." Hanging up, Maddie told Rick, "Janie says to go home and relax. Tomorrow's another day, and she has a new case for us! Let's get you back at CPS and your car," she said cheerfully.

"Okay. Um, Maddie?" He stopped walking and faced her. "I just want to thank you for letting me tag along this afternoon. It was very educational and a big relief after going out with Monica this morning. I was beginning to think I was in the wrong job, that CPS wasn't what I thought it was, that I had miscalculated somehow."

"What did you think it was?"

"A place to advocate for children, to show compassion, to provide answers and programs to help parents find a better way to discipline their children, and to be happier with their lives."

Maddie smiled. "It's all that and more, Rick. But each caseworker brings his or her own personality to the job. You've seen how Monica handles her cases and how I handle mine. If you get a chance to go out with other workers, you'll find they have their own unique style, too."

"I'm not sure about Monica's style, frankly," he admitted.

"She's great on making sure all the dots are dotted and the T's crossed. She's had some successful cases, Rick. It's mostly her attitude that sucks. But from what Janie said, everything you did at the Durants' was appropriate and professional in spite of Monica. I'm just glad you weren't intimidated by her."

"I kind of was," he told her sheepishly.

"But it didn't stop you from doing what needed to be done for Mimi. That's the important thing." Maddie smiled at him. "You did very well, Rick."

She took him back to CPS, aware of how she felt when she was near him and trying not to show it. He gave her a smart salute as he closed her car door and whistled a happy tune as he headed for his car.

CHAPTER 4

New Case

IT DAWNED COLD AND raw the next morning and Maddie shivered. She had time to eat some breakfast with her parents and sat and visited with them.

"I've heard all about the Durants," said Lucy Roper, her red curly hair still mussed and tangled from sleep, and she chatted about everything she'd heard.

Maddie smiled, then frowned and interrupted her mother. "Some of those details are wrong, Mom. It didn't happen exactly like that. Dawn has not been removed from the parents permanently; she's in temporary foster care. She will go back home when the judge feels the parents are ready. Nor is she pregnant, that we know of. She was only assaulted two days ago. Please, it's essential that you do not talk about the Durant situation or that CPS is involved with them. That's confidential information. If they knew their friends at church knew about this, they'd be embarrassed unnecessarily."

Roper patted Maddie's hand. "We've only been listening to what people tell us, but we don't confirm or deny what they're saying."

"Please tell them the information about the Durants is strictly confidential and to keep it to themselves." Looking over at her mother, Maddie noticed she looked offended.

"I would never gossip about such a thing, Mads! It hurts that you think I would."

Sitting back, Maddie offered her apologies but she wondered if her mother, who was known to have a hard time keeping secrets, actually did keep her mouth shut. Maddie did her best to give her the benefit of the doubt and although it took a while, her mother finally calmed down.

A bad start to the day, thought Maddie later as she got in her car to go to work. Besides the new case, she had three visits to make, two hearings, and a permanency plan for the Durants to draw up. First thing on the agenda was setting up a visit between Dawn and her mother.

Rick was already in when she got there, talking with some of the other workers on the team. He smiled when he saw her and broke away from the group to follow her to her office.

"Are you an early bird by nature?" she asked him, smiling.

"I guess. Army life will do that to you," he told her. "What's on the agenda for today?"

Maddie dropped her briefcase down and shed her coat and scarf. "Nippy out there," she commented, then plopped in her chair. "'The agenda for the day,'" she quoted him. "You're all business this morning. How about let's talk about yesterday first? I'd like to get your thoughts and feelings about the visits we made and the court hearing. What did you observe? What did you think worked well? What could have gone better?"

"Ah, a debriefing. You want to pick my brain."

"We'll both benefit. I'll learn what I'm doing well and what I can improve. You'll learn what to look for to put in your reports when you write up your own visits with your kids and parents and your monthly progress reports."

"Sounds like you're all business now," Rick commented dryly.

"Wait until we get to the permanency plan for the families! That's serious business. This 'debriefing' is just for us. So, let's begin with your overall impression of the visits yesterday. Start with the Harpers, Dom and Eunice. What were your impressions of them and how I dealt with them?"

Rick sat for a moment, reflecting. He pictured the couple in his mind. "Okay," he began, "Dom first. Sometimes he wasn't very cooperative, kind of mocking in his tone, and other times he seemed to be cooperating, though I'm not sure if he was sincere or not. It almost seemed like he didn't want his wife to succeed but she is certainly determined to. My question is, what if she succeeds but Dom doesn't? Do the kids go home, or not?"

"Good question. That's every worker's dilemma. My personal opinion is that Dom will never stop drinking and, in that case, Eunice will need to make a decision about whether to stay with her husband and lose her two boys, or leave him and get her boys back."

"So, what are you going to do?"

"Wait and see for now. They have a hearing coming up in a couple of weeks and it should be clear by then which way Eunice will lean."

Rick nodded thoughtfully. "It's certainly not as clear cut as in the Army where you shape up or you get shipped out. You can't threaten a civilian client like you can a soldier."

"Right. We don't have that kind of authority. That's why CPS is more like a response to abuse rather than a preventer of abuse. Kind of sad, isn't it?"

"Yeah."

"Did I do anything right during that visit?" asked Maddie. Rick wondered if she were fishing for compliments, then realized she wasn't.

"I thought you were clear with Dom that he was part of the problem, not the solution, and I felt you were very encouraging to Eunice. She looked sober to me yesterday."

"Thank you. What could I have done differently or better?"

Rick was again surprised by her question. "Frankly," he told her, "I thought you handled both of them well. You were polite and tolerant of Dom and without appearing to take sides, you were able to encourage Eunice. I'd give you an 'A' on that visit."

Maddie blushed and laughed. "You're just trying to butter me up," she teased. "But, seriously, thanks. We can only do our best, though it won't always come out the way we want. What about the other two visits?"

More confidently, Rick gave her his impressions and a suggestion or two which she accepted gladly, and then they talked about the Browns' court case and getting their kids back.

"A happy ending. We live for them here."

"Most aren't?"

"Most aren't," she agreed sadly. "New abuse reports keep popping up on our clients repeatedly. But, let's not get into that now. No sense discouraging you in your first week on the job. Let's go get some coffee and whatever's left over to eat in the break room." She stood up in readiness and Rick followed suit.

Later, just before they were getting ready to leave for a visit and then a court hearing, Janie came to Maddie's office.

"I have the new case for you two," she said. "It's a military case sent to us from a base in Germany and since Rick's been in the Army, I thought he would be an asset in dealing with this family. Read the file over and try to contact the family sometime today. Essentially, the father viciously beat the daughter with a belt and the school bus driver noticed she was crying and had a hard time sitting still and asked her what was wrong. He took her to the school nurse and the authorities were contacted. This is a black couple with an only child. I'm sure you'll both do well working with this family."

Out in Maddie's car on the way to her visit with the Berman family Maddie proposed they keep the visit short, contact the new family, the Ordmans, and squeeze a visit in with them between the court hearing and lunch. Rick had no objections.

Fortunately, the Berman visit never happened because Mrs. Berman had an unexpected dental appointment for a broken tooth and Mr. Berman drove her because she didn't drive due to a seizure disorder. Back out in the car, Maddie called the Ordmans. They told her to come out any time so they drove right over there.

George Ordman was a dark-skinned, strongly muscled man, but fear showed in his eyes when he saw Maddie and Rick at the door. He invited them in nervously. His wife, Amelia, joined them in the living room and gestured for them all to sit. She was lighter skinned than her husband, a little on the stout side, and she stared at Maddie and Rick with pursed lips.

"Mr. and Mrs. Ordman," Maddie began, keeping her voice calm and pleasant, "this is my partner, Rick Shelby, and I am Madison Roper, Maddie for short. We're with Child Protective Services and we're here to work with you on reuniting you with your daughter—Clarissa, is it?"

"Yes," answered Amelia Ordman. "When can we see her?"

"We'll be arranging that as soon as we go to court. The judge decides when and where you'll meet her. But we need to talk about a few other things first." Maddie then led them into telling about what happened in Germany that led them to get so angry and beat Clarissa. Basically, George Ordman explained, Clarissa, nine-years old, had talked back to her mother, saying, "No, I don't want to!" The mother started slapping Clarissa and Ordman, coming into the kitchen, asked what was going on. When he found out, he pulled off his belt and started beating Clarissa all over. He hung his head when he finished talking.

"I didn't mean to hurt her so bad," he said, "but she wouldn't stand still, and I lost my temper and just kept hitting her."

"If she hadn't sassed me," said Amelia, "none of this would have happened. Now our whole life is in ruins because of her!"

"No, Mrs. Ordman, Clarissa is not the cause of your problems. You're here now because the both of you lost control and hurt Clarissa," Maddie corrected gently.

"My husband has been discharged from the Army and has no job, and I'm pregnant!" said the woman as if she hadn't heard Maddie. "What do we do now? The Army found this apartment for us but look at it! It's awful! The paint's peeling, the faucet drips, the hot water doesn't work." Her lips turned down in disgust.

Ordman put a calming hand on his wife's arm, then turned to Maddie and Rick. "I'm in the process of getting a job lined up as a mechanic and will start hopefully on Monday," he told them, "and I put in an application for one of those new homes going up just outside of town." He turned to Maddie and asked quietly, "What will we have to do to get our girl back?"

"We'll set up a permanency plan for you and Amelia, which will outline what the judge will order you to do to get Clarissa back. Clarissa will be placed in an appropriate foster home—I have a good one in mind for her, and Rick and I will visit her at least weekly. We'll also arrange for parent-child visits for you after we go to court and the judge determines where and how often you'll meet. You'll probably be ordered to take parenting and anger management classes as well. Those are the main things. If the judge orders other things we'll make arrangements for them too. Mrs. Ordman, I hope you'll see a doctor regarding your pregnancy." She nodded that she would.

"Please call us George and Amelia," said Ordman. "And I promise, we will do everything the judge orders us to do to get Clarissa back,"

"Thank you. I'm Maddie and this is Rick. Do you have any other questions for us?" Maddie asked.

"No," said Ordman. "I just can't tell you how sorry I am I hurt my daughter so badly."

"I hope you tell her that when you see her, George," Maddie told him quietly. "It would go a long way to healing the emotional hurt."

"Have you seen Clarissa yet?" asked Amelia.

"No, we haven't. We just got the case an hour ago. But I will do my best to see her either today or tomorrow."

"Tomorrow's Saturday. Do you work on Saturdays too?"

"Often," laughed Maddie. She stood up and the others did too. "Thank you for meeting with us. I will be in touch with you early next week to begin drawing up your permanency plan. The court hearing is usually ten days after a report is filed so it will be the following week."

"No visits until then?" asked Ordman.

"No, sir, I'm sorry." He looked like a defeated man, but she was pleased he felt remorse for what he'd done. That was a positive sign. As for the mother, she couldn't quite get a reading on her.

Out in the car, Maddie drove for a while, then pulled over to the curb to fill out her mileage sheet and jot a few notes. Rick found himself more and more impressed with her kindness and the respect she showed to all the families she'd visited. How different from Monica Tubbs, he thought. It was going to be a pleasure learning how CPS worked from Maddie.

"Okay," she said, stashing the forms in her door pocket. "Let's get to the court hearing and afterwards we'll find a restaurant and discuss the Ordmans over lunch. How's that sound to you?"

"Great."

At the fast food restaurant, while they ate their cheeseburgers, Maddie asked Rick to tell her about how the military identifies and deals with child abuse.

"From what I understand, there's a Point of Contact who receives reports of child abuse. If the Abuse Team determines the abuse will continue, the child is removed to a temporary foster home until they determine what course of action to take. If the soldier did the abuse, he and the family are usually relocated to a city with a military base nearby. I think a social worker accompanies the family to their new location in the States where a place is found for the parents to live and the child is placed with Child Protective Services. That's the extent of my knowledge, which may even be out-of-date. Betty, my ex-wife, explained it to me one time."

"Thanks, that was helpful. Now tell me what you thought of my interview with the parents."

"One thing I really liked was when you called Mrs. Ordman on blaming Clarissa for their current circumstances. You made it clear, but nicely, that it was their own lack of self-control that caused it."

"Thanks. It was hard for me at first to be that forthright with abusive parents, but it's essential that they realize that they're the adults and they're the ones who must change their discipline methods. Clarissa is just a child who will naturally push the boundaries, as all children do. However, I think it was a harsher beating than she'd ever gotten before because Ordman really lost it. I see mom as unrelenting in some ways but dad more lenient, despite having lost it with Clarissa. He was certainly remorseful, and my guess is he will cooperate with us fully, while mom may fight us."

"That's how I would sum it up, too."

"Okay! Well, onward and upward. Now we have two foster home visits and a hearing, so let's get going. I want to get a visit arranged for tomorrow if I can, for Dawn and Mimi Durant also. Ready?"

"Yup." They grabbed their coats and hurried through the wind to the car.

"Brrrr," grumbled Maddie as she slid into her car seat. "Perfect day to stay in the office and write reports but there's no time today. Right now, we're going to visit three children who were abused by their dad when he got chewed out by his First

Sergeant and came home drunk and took his frustrations out on them. The younger boy got knocked down by the dad and cut his head, so the children were removed when the mother refused to protect her kids from her husband. The kids' names are Cory, an eight-year old red head, Julie, six, and Mikey, four. The parents are David and Mary Stuart, who are reluctantly attending parenting classes, plus AA for David. They're not very cooperative. David is an Army Private at Fort Carson. He was a Private First Class but got bumped back to an E1 because of the abuse. You can help me with this case. The mother, Mary, is a spitfire, small, wiry, and snappy. She's a she-bear!"

Rick laughed at the description. "Are we going to see them now?" he asked.

"No, just the kids. They're homesick but doing alright."

They pulled up at the foster home several minutes later.

"Hi, Emma," Maddie greeted the foster mother, Emma Watkins, who grinned at her, nodded at Rick, and urged them to hurry inside out of the cold. "How are you doing? How are the Stuart kids doing?" asked Maddie.

In answer to her question, the three little Stuarts came rushing into the living room.

"Hi, Maddie!" they chorused together, and tossed themselves onto her lap and into her arms. Cory and Julie chattered to her about the friends they were making in the neighborhood and school, while Mickey just wanted to crawl in her lap and nestle. She kissed him and listened to the other two until they ran out of things to say.

"It's so good to see you guys are happy here. Your foster mom's special. She was able to take in the three of you so you could stay together. So, you're very lucky."

"Yeah!" agreed the three kids, who then showered Emma with hugs.

Grinning at the kids, Maddie asked them, "Would you three mind if I have a word with Emma alone?" The older two nodded their heads and took Mikey's hand and they sauntered slowly out of the room.

"They like you, Maddie. I don't always see that reaction with children and their caseworkers. You're doing a good job for them."

"Thanks, Emma. Emma, I'd like you to meet a new worker at CPS. This is Rick Shelby, Rick this is Emma Watkins."

Rick reached over and shook her hand. "Nice to meet you. Mrs. Watkins," he said with a smile.

"Please, call me Emma. All the caseworkers do. Hope you like working for CPS, Rick. I know you'll enjoy working with Maddie. She's one of the best."

"So I'm finding out," he replied. Maddie blushed at the double compliment and then steered them toward the business at hand: the Stuart children. Emma told how they were resistant and scared at first, Mikey crying for his mother all the time, but that after a few days they had settled in and were doing much better. Mikey and Julie were good eaters, but Cory seemed to have a nervous stomach, often complaining that it hurt. Maddie called the office and arranged for an assistant to take Cory to a doctor to have it checked out.

After hugs and handshakes, Maddie and Rick left for another foster home visit.

In the car Maddie explained, "We're on our way to see Candace Aberdeen next, a fifteen-year old who was kicked out of her house for being involved with satanism. Candy claims to have been kidnapped and taken to a coven and raped repeatedly before being released. She says she wandered around for hours, afraid to go home. When she did go home, she tried to tell her mother what happened, but her mom didn't believe her. However, after Candy took seven showers inside of two hours and cried all night long, the mother began to believe that something had happened and called CPS. When the caseworker got there, the mom told her to take Candy away, she didn't want 'that filth' in her home. So Candy was removed because of mom's refusal to protect."

At the Elena Menendez foster home, Maddie and Rick visited with Candy, who was sullen and depressed looking, answered questions in monosyllables, and seemed to have lost interest in life. Maddie felt the girl could benefit from counseling with a therapist specializing in sexual trauma and abuse cases.

"Candy?" she ventured and waited for her to look at her. When she did, Maddie explained what she would like to do and asked, "Would you let me set you up with one?"

Candy eyes filled with tears. "Please," she whispered. "I can't sleep at night and when I do, I have nightmares. I'm afraid to leave the house, afraid to go to school. I just can't stop thinking about it."

"I'll arrange it right away, Candy." Maddie scooted over to her and hugged her. Candy leaned into her and cried.

In talking with Elena a few minutes later, Maddie shared what had transpired.

"That's the first she's opened up to anyone," Elena said. "I'm so grateful you're her caseworker."

"Thank you. I'll be in touch."

Rick was enthusiastic when they got out in the car. "You are amazing!" he told her. "I'm so glad I'm training with you."

"She was ready to accept help, Rick. I just happened to be there and say the right words at the right time."

Grinning to himself he gave her credit for two more things, following attractive, kind, caring, and giving. She also took advantage of a teaching moment when a person was ready to receive help and being genuinely modest. His estimation of Maddie Roper rose several more notches.

At the end of the day as they finished making arrangements for getting Dawn and Mimi together for a visit tomorrow, Maddie turned to Rick with a pensive look in her eyes.

"What's up?" he asked.

She grinned sheepishly and said, “I was wondering if you’d be willing to help me move into my new apartment this weekend. Jaime, from Intake, is going to help and I thought two guys would be better than one.”

“Ah, you want my muscles!” he joked good-naturedly. “Sure, I’d be glad to. Where are you staying now?”

“With my parents in the parsonage. I don’t have that much stuff, but it’s time to move out and give them their space back.”

He looked at her quizzically a moment. “May I ask why you’re still living at home?”

“Bad marriage ending in divorce. I moved back home eighteen months ago, but it’s time to get on with my life.”

He nodded. “Just tell me where and when and I’ll be there.”

“The parsonage right next to the church. Ten o’clock.”

CHAPTER 5

Moving Out

MADDIE CONTACTED JOAN PEREZ, her youth group assistant, later that evening and after fifteen minutes of pleasantries Maddie asked if the other apartment in her building was still for rent. Joan squealed with delight.

"Yes, the apartment is still available! I'll tell the manager right away that you're interested. When would you be moving over here?"

"Tomorrow?" replied Maddie uncertainly. "Once I made up my mind, it's like I want to do it right away. Do you think tomorrow's too soon to plan for? I've got a couple of guys from work who will help me move."

"Let me talk to the manager and I'll get right back to you."

Joan clicked off and not five minutes later called Maddie back to tell her the good news. The apartment was available and had just recently been cleaned, so she could move in any time.

"Great!" exclaimed Maddie. "The guys will be here at 10:00 tomorrow morning so we'll be arriving over there before noon. Thanks for everything, Joan. I better go and break the news to my parents—"

"They don't know yet? You're brave, Maddie, dropping it on them so suddenly, especially your mother."

"I know. We'll see how it goes. They're probably ready and willing for me to leave so they can have their privacy again." As she closed her phone, she lost some of her excitement. Joan's comment rattled her. She was really remiss in not informing her parents sooner about this move.

She hurried down the stairs to the living room where her parents were catching the news on the television. She stopped abruptly in front of them and cleared her throat. Both looked at her questioningly and Roper turned the volume down.

"I have some news and I'm sorry about not warning you sooner," she began, getting nervous about their reaction. "I've decided to move into an apartment of my own finally, and-and it's going to happen tomorrow morning. There's a vacant apartment in Joan's building," she rushed on, "and I'm going to move in there."

"I see," said Roper slowly, glancing at his wife.

"Oh, Mads!" exclaimed Lucy. "Have we offended you somehow? Hurt your feelings? I love having you live here with us. Do you have to leave so quickly?" A deep frown appeared on her forehead. Maddie went to her mother and hugged her.

"You haven't done anything wrong, Mom, neither of you have. It's just that it's been eighteen months and I think I need to move on with my life. I'll only be three blocks away, and I'll probably be over all the time to see you anyway, plus I'll see you at church every week. It's just that, it's time. Please understand."

She stood back from Lucy and searched both parents' faces. Roper and Lucy looked at each other, assessing this new development. Roper was the first to make a decision. He stood and embraced Maddie.

"You know we love you with all our hearts, Mads. If this is what you really want to do at this time and feel ready to venture out on your own, then we'll support you 100%." He turned to

Lucy for confirmation but she barely nodded, worry written all over her face.

"I'm just afraid you'll find another Joe Skeeter and lose another baby," she said.

"Oh, Mom!" said Maddie in despair. "That will never happen again!"

Lucy dabbed at tears and was clearly not convinced. "We love you so much, Mads. You're safe here. I want you to stay. I don't want you to move away or marry another jerk."

"I'm not moving away, Mom. I'm not even looking for a new husband. I just think I've overstayed my welcome here and that you two need your privacy back. I feel ready to get my own apartment now and move forward with my life."

Lucy remained unrelenting.

"You two have been so good to me. You took me back in all battered and broken and put me back together again. You nursed me through the loss of my baby. You've done a wonderful job, Mom! Please, let me do this without making me feel guilty."

Lucy stiffened, then realized that what Maddie was saying was true. She was laying a guilt trip on her. She closed her eyes and took several deep breaths.

"Okay, Mads, I won't fight you any more, but you have to promise me you'll call me every day and have Sunday dinner here with us every week."

"I promise, Mom, I will!"

Finally, Lucy collected herself, accepting the inevitable. "Well, then," she said, "if you're set on doing this, how can we help you get ready for this move?" Maddie's heart swelled. That was her mother, laying guilt trips one minute, offering to help the next.

"I need to pack, of course. I need to decide what to borrow from you for a while, like any of your old pots and pans, dishes, towels, you know, that kind of stuff. I brought nothing back with me from Pueblo so I'm going to have to buy furniture for the apartment." Maddie was getting more excited about moving now that her mother was going to help.

"I have an extra set of dishes and silverware I can give you, some kitchen towels, a towel or two for the bathroom. You've got your bedroom furniture you can take and your desk and bookshelf. We just need to gather these things together and arrange them in the hallway for tomorrow. Is anyone coming to help you?"

"Two guys from work."

"Well, then, let's get to work!"

Lucy masterminded the packing operation downstairs, Roper obediently doing everything she told him to do. Meanwhile, Maddie went upstairs to pack up her clothes, toiletries, and computer. She cleared out the desk and filing cabinet and put everything into boxes. It took the rest of the evening and the next morning to get everything ready.

Jaime and Rick arrived at 10:00 sharp the next morning to transport her things over to the new apartment. Her apartment was arranged like Joan's, which she'd been in several times, so she had a pretty good idea of where her things would go. The guys did a wonderful job carrying the stuff up a flight of stairs without complaint or mishap. She rewarded them with pizza for lunch, but they had to sit on the floor because the one thing she didn't have was a kitchen table or chairs. Jaime left after they ate because he had made plans to take his children to a movie.

"What now?" asked Rick. "Unpacking?"

"That and I need to buy a table and chairs," she answered.

"I'll go with you if you want," he offered.

"Really? Great! How about right now?"

"Sure," he said rising and grabbing her hand, lifting her up, too. Maddie smiled at him and became aware that her heart was thumping a little harder than before he grabbed her hand.

At the mall, Maddie fell in love with the first dinette set she saw. It sat four, but that was all she needed, so she bought it and Rick helped her load it in her car. Then they went back inside the mall to look at television sets, a couch and armchairs, an end table and lamps. Finally, feeling like she's spent her wad and then some, she called it quits.

Back at the apartment, Rick helped her set the table up and then hooked up the TV. The rest would arrive next week. Tired, they both plopped on the kitchen chairs.

"Rick, I can't thank you enough for your help today. I need to pay you, or something, for your time and all your hard work."

He looked at her, his eyes twinkling. "The only pay I'd like is for you to go out to dinner with me some time this coming week. I know you'll be busy getting unpacked and set up here, but maybe by next Friday you'll be able to."

As flattered as Maddie was, flashes of Joe wining and dining her in the beginning of their relationship clouded her vision momentarily. But she smiled, hoping Rick hadn't seen the hesitation.

"I'd love to, Rick," she told him. "Thank you." Rick stood then, smiling at her. He had seen the hesitation but dismissed it, for now. Maybe someday he'd find out what it was about.

"Okay, then, Maddie. I'll leave you now to the fun part of moving in, all the unpacking and then all the arranging and rearranging."

Maddie laughed and swatted playfully at his arm. "Oh," she said, jumping up. "I need to drive you over to your car at the parsonage."

"Nah, don't bother. It's only a couple of blocks away. I'll hoof it. I need the exercise." They both laughed as Maddie walked him to the door.

Closing the door behind him she stood there a moment, contemplating his invitation to dinner. Was she ready to get back in the dating game? Move out on her own on one day, start dating a week later? Kind of rushing it, she thought. She wanted to get used to living on her own before tackling anything else new. On the other hand, Rick was such a sweet guy, not to mention good-looking, helpful, and a Christian. Compared to Joe, he was an angel.

She went back into her kitchen and made a cup of tea, sitting at her new table and relaxing for a few minutes. Then she rose and went into her bedroom and started to unpack, remembering and chuckling at Rick's comment about arranging and rearranging. Everything was pretty much in order as the time approached 5:00.

Her stomach growled. Well, with no food in the house there was only one thing to do. She called her parents and invited herself over for dinner. Good sports that they were, they told her to come on over. She told them all about the fun she'd had moving in and unpacking, as well as Rick's invitation to go out dinner with him as payment for helping her all day.

"But keep that a secret for now," she told them. "I may delay it because I don't want to rush into another relationship before I get to know Rick better." Lucy, as expected, frowned, but Roper smiled; he knew and liked Rick.

Sunday morning dawned cold, overcast, and snowy. Maddie sat up in bed and for a moment she didn't know where she was. As she looked around at the empty boxes strewn everywhere, though, the realization hit her, and with a grin, she jumped out of bed and twirled around. Noting the time, she hurried and showered and got dressed for church. She wanted to get to church early and grab a bite to eat; they always had pastries and coffee available, sometimes fruit, and occasionally scrambled eggs.

As luck would have it, this morning there were egg casseroles, biscuits and coffee. She grabbed a plate and hurried into the youth room to teach her Sunday school class. She had fourteen youngsters today. Dawn Durant, as expected, was absent. Maddie smiled at the group. She loved that it was made up of blacks, whites, Asians, and Mexicans. As far as Maddie could tell, they were all good friends and she was immensely proud of them. During the church service, Maddie sang with the choir. Afterwards, she met and chatted with her mother for a while.

"I was thinking about your upcoming date with Rick," commented Lucy. "Are you sure that's wise, dear?"

"What do you mean?"

"Well, Joe started out wining and dining you and you were smitten and looked what happened there."

Maddie bit her tongue, then chose her words carefully. "Mom, Rick is 100% different from Joe. He's a member here in our church, he advocates for children at CPS, he was very helpful yesterday in helping me move in and buy furniture. He's a kind, thoughtful person, Mom. Anyway, it's just one dinner date. He was so helpful yesterday and wouldn't accept any payment, I just felt it would be alright to go out to dinner with him." Lucy's worried look finally resolved itself.

"You're right, Mads. It's just that I don't want to see you get hurt again."

"I know, Mom. But it'll be alright, I promise."

They parted and went to their separate cars then. The snow had virtually stopped but unfortunately had frozen on the windshield. Maddie began to scrape the windshield off when Rick approached her and took the scraper away from her.

"I've got longer arms," he explained grinning and finished clearing the ice away so she could see to drive.

"Why, thank you, kind sir," she said, matching his grin.

Lucy Roper came over to them, a bright smile on her face. Looking at Rick she asked what he was doing for Sunday dinner.

"Um, nothing special, Mrs. Roper," he replied.

"Good, why don't you join us, then? You don't mind, Mads, do you?" she asked.

"Not at all! I think it's a great idea. It'll give you a chance to get to know each other. Besides, we're having roast chicken today and Mom is an outstanding cook." Rick hesitated briefly, sensing some tension between the two women, but since Maddie was agreeable to it he decided to accept.

"Thank you. I'd be delighted," he told Lucy Roper.

As predicted, the dinner was delicious. Then while dessert was being served, the Ropers began to ask Rick lots of questions about himself. They didn't explain why. Rick sensed they were checking him out and answered all their questions. From the tone of the questions, he surmised Maddie had been hurt by her ex-husband. He'd ask Maddie at a later time. Apparently satisfied with Rick's answers, Roper sat back and asked what his hobbies were.

"Well, I'm into physical fitness. I like to hike up mountains and work out regularly in the gym," he answered. "I'm also into conservation and saving the environment, and helping people out of jams, which led me to get the job at CPS."

Maddie chuckled. "He also likes clearing ice off windshields for short damsels in distress!"

"I saw that," commented Lucy. "I'm sure she appreciated it. Also, I hear you two have a dinner date on Friday."

Maddie blushed, her eyes briefly flashing anger at her mother.

Rick caught the look and kept his tone light. "She wanted to pay me for helping her move yesterday so I asked her to join me for dinner instead," he explained. "She said yes so I didn't think I was out of line."

"No, of course not," Lucy answered quickly, flustered by the look in Maddie's eyes. Then she remembered she wasn't supposed to say anything.

Maddie stood up. "I really need to get back to my apartment and finish unpacking. It's already 2:00 and I also need to go grocery shopping. I'll help you clean off the table and then I'll be on my way."

"I'll help your mother, Mads," Roper said. "You can go on and do what you need to do." He smiled at her and drew her close, hugging her. “Don’t be upset,” he whispered. “Your mother didn’t mean anything by saying that.”

Maddie hugged her father back and tried to relax. She felt embarrassed to even look at Rick now. He’d want to know what her anger was all about and she didn’t want to explain her mother’s over protectiveness because of Joe. How would she be able to work with him at CPS and go out to dinner with him on Friday without feeling so embarrassed? Darn interfering mothers!

Pulling away from her dad, Maddie said, “Okay, then, I’ll call you in a day or two.” She ignored her mother’s stricken look and Rick’s penetrating eyes and headed for her coat and then the door. Rick thanked the Ropers for the dinner, retrieved his coat and followed Maddie out quickly. Neither of them was aware that Lucy Roper broke down in tears after they left and needed to be consoled by her husband.

Maddie was getting into her car when Rick hollered to her to wait up. She rolled her window down so they could talk but she wouldn’t look at him when he came over.

“Do you want to talk about what just happened?” he asked her, leaning in the window. She shook her head no, still looking down. “Maddie, I think we should, otherwise it’s going to hang between us and cause problems.” Maddie teared up. As soon as Rick saw the tears, he scurried around to the passenger side of the car and got in. Maddie quickly rolled her window up, shivering.

“Drive a couple of blocks away,” he told her quietly. Obediently, Maddie drove a couple of blocks until she found an open parking spot and stopped. Rick turned toward her.

“I’m sorry, Rick,” she mumbled. “My mom has a habit of interfering in my life. She’s afraid I’ll make another mistake in marrying the wrong guy so she’s hyper about who I see or date. She wants to vet everyone first. I made the mistake of mentioning our date on Friday. That’s why she invited you over to dinner, to rake you over the coals. Dad thinks the world of you, but Mom is so suspicious. She doesn't trust anyone!"

"Maddie, both of your parents love you, there's absolutely no doubt about that. They each show it in different ways. Your mom is very protective; that's her way of showing it. I understand now why they asked me so many questions; they were checking me out, comparing me to your ex. I get that. My concern is how you reacted back there. You can barely look me in the eye. Why? Did I say something wrong?"

"No, of course not!" she said, finally looking at him.

"I want us to continue working together, Maddie. If going out to dinner next Friday complicates things, then let's not go. I'm probably rushing things anyway. It's just that in the three days I've worked with you, I've been impressed with the kind of person you are, your passion for helping people, especially children, and your faith. But you may not be ready yet to date after what I gather was a disastrous marriage."

Despite her best intentions, Maddie began to cry in earnest. Rick scooted as close to her as he could get with the console between them and reached his arm around her. She leaned into him. They stayed that way until Maddie was cried out. Finally sitting back in her seat, Maddie wiped her face, blew her nose, and took a deep breath.

"I'm sorry, Rick," she said. "It's the first time I've cried since leaving Joe and losing my baby."

"You lost your baby?" asked Rick, shocked. "Because of your ex?" Maddie nodded. "Can you talk about it?"

"Joe was drunk and when I told him I was pregnant, he hit me and knocked me down and then kicked me in the stomach. As soon as he passed out on the couch I drove straight home to Mom and Dad, but I started hemorrhaging on the way and was rushed to the hospital as soon as I got here. I probably can't have any more kids." She teared up again.

Rick absorbed that information then told her, "I would never hurt you, Maddie. I'm not a violent man; I'm a protector by nature. But I guess I better let you and your parents get to know me more."

"For your information, Joe started out sweet and charming just like you. We were all taken in by him. Mom and dad gave their blessing to our marriage and it was after that, when we were on our own, that he started to change. We lived in Colorado Springs at first and I worked for an adoption agency. Then he lost his job and wanted to move to Pueblo, but the job he thought he had there didn't pan out. That's when the drinking started. And the jealousy. He became so controlling. I had no support system in Pueblo and he didn't want me working. I tried to get involved in a church but he made such a ruckus that I stopped going. Then I got pregnant and I was so happy. I was sure that would make him happy, too, but it didn't. It enraged him. When I sneaked out of the house after the beating, I knew I would lose the baby." Maddie paused and sighed. "Listen to me!" she said, "I sound just like some of the women on my caseload who are abused by their husbands."

"It makes you more sensitive to them," commented Rick quietly. His heart hurt for her.

She looked at him. "Now you know my story, but it stays between us, okay? Only Janie knows at work and Joan, my best friend from church. As for us working together, I don't see a problem as long as we act professional. As for next Friday evening, let's wait and see how the week goes, okay?"

Rick nodded. "Sure. I won't tell another soul. I appreciate you telling me your story, Maddie. And I'm glad we'll still be able to work together. Friday night, I assure you, can be rescheduled as you see fit or even cancelled. That'll be your call."

Maddie smiled at him. "Thanks. You seem like a such good person. Don't change on me like Joe did." She let out a big sigh "Ready to go back and get your car now?"

"If you're ready."

"Yes, I'm ready. I'll go home and finish unpacking, then go grocery shopping. That will put time and distance between today's dinner with Mom and Dad and the rest of my life."

"You're going to do okay, Maddie. You're a strong woman." She squeezed Rick's hand in gratitude.

CHAPTER 6

Skeeter

THINGS WENT BETTER AT work than Maddie expected. Rick was professional but still his same pleasant, charming self. On visits, he quickly picked up the tell-tale signs of lying when clients denied using drugs or insisted their children got a black eye and split lip from a fall. He was observant, sensitive, and kind. In short, he was a wonderful partner. Too bad they wouldn't always be able to work together, mused Maddie, but once he got his own caseload there just wouldn't be time. Maddie kept Janie abreast of how well Rick was doing.

"That's good," commented Janie, "because Roger Burns is leaving us soon and I was hoping to give some of his cases to Rick. In fact, I was thinking of letting Rick go out with Roger for the next couple of weeks to become familiar with his cases." Janie watched Maddie for her reaction and chuckled. "You like Rick, don't you? I know he certainly likes you and is impressed with how you work with your clients."

Maddie blushed. "He's a very nice man," she said.

"Has he asked you out yet?"

More blushing: "A dinner date tomorrow."

"Trust him," Janie told her. "All my senses tell me he's a good person with high moral standards. He won't hurt you."

Maddie smiled back at Janie. "Thank you for reassuring me. I guess I'm still a little gun-shy."

"Understandably. Tell you what, if at any point on your date with Rick you feel uncomfortable or feel he's getting too pushy or demanding, you call me at home right away; you have my number. I don't think that will happen but if it will make you feel safer, call me. Agreed?"

"Agreed!" She went over to Janie and gave her a hug. "Thank you for caring."

"My pleasure. Got to watch out for all my children!" Janie was in her late fifties and consistently thought of herself as the mother of all the younger workers. Maddie felt blessed to have Janie as her supervisor.

Later that day, Marcia, her team's secretary, came to Maddie's office and announced she had a visitor.

"A client?" asked Maddie, rising to go out and get the visitor.

"I don't think so. His name is Joe Skeeter." Maddie froze. Joe Skeeter, her ex? Why was he here?

"Marcia," she said quietly. "Please tell him I don't want to see him and for him to leave."

"Is something wrong, Maddie?"

"Please just tell him."

Marcia nodded and headed out to relay the message. Maddie stood at her door listening and heard Joe's voice rising in volume as he argued with Marcia, demanding to know which office was Maddie's and insisting on talking with her. There was enough of a commotion going on that workers stopped what they were doing to watch or came out from their offices to investigate, including Janie. Janie figured out right away it was Joe Skeeter and marched up to him and told him to leave the premises. Maddie heard him stomp off and sat down, shaking. Janie sent everyone back to their offices then went to see Maddie.

"I'm sorry," Maddie began. "I had no idea he was in town or that he knew where I worked."

"How are you going to handle him?" asked Janie as she closed the door and sat by Maddie's desk.

"At the moment, I'm not sure. I'm just praying he hasn't found out where I live."

"You're not with your parents anymore?"

"No, I just moved out last Saturday into an apartment of my own."

Janie thought a moment. "Do you have a restraining order on him?"

"Yes, it was included in the divorce decree."

"Then call the police if he shows up at your apartment or he starts stalking you. No delays, no hesitations, just call them immediately."

Maddie nodded, her brain swirling with memories of the beating and losing her baby. Her fear of Joe turned her stomach to acid and she wanted to throw up.

Janie stood. "I'm going to make you a cup of tea," she said. "Sit and try to relax until I get back." Maddie did as she was told, closing her eyes and trying to breathe deeply to ease the turmoil in her stomach. Janie returned a few minutes later with the tea.

"I have a hearing," said Maddie.

"Does Rick know the case?"

"Yes, we just saw the kids and the parents yesterday."

"Good, no time like the present for him to get his feet wet in court. Think you're up to coaching him a bit before he goes?""

"I think so."

Rick came to her office and Maddie did her best to tell him which key points to make in his testimony. It was the Berman case, which was going well. Basically, it was a progress report on their attendance at parenting classes.

"Okay," said Rick when she was done, "now tell me why you're not going."

"Upset stomach. I'm trying to relax with a cup of tea. You'll do fine, Rick."

"What's the upset stomach from?" he persisted. Maddie, as far as he could tell, was a healthy, well-adjusted woman. What would cause her to get a bad stomach ache? He vaguely wondered if the commotion he'd heard out by the secretary's waiting area had anything to do with it, but he hadn't been able to hear what was said so wasn't sure. She shook her head, took a sip of tea, sat back, and closed her eyes. Rick got the hint and quietly left her office.

When it was time to go home, Maddie checked to see if Joe were hanging around outside the building and was relieved that she didn't see him anywhere. Still, she made sure she walked out with several other workers and made it safely to her car. Fortunately, her stomach had settled down and all she wanted to do now was go home and relax. Pulling into a parking slot reserved for her apartment, she checked around the lot, feeling afraid and paranoid that Joe knew where she lived. But she didn't see him, nor the Silverado he drove, anywhere. Taking a breath and hurrying to the door, she let herself in and headed for her second floor apartment.

Inside she finally relaxed, removed her coat and gloves, and headed for the kitchen to get a glass of water. Get a grip, Maddie, you're safe here, she told herself. Then she got the idea of calling Joan and inviting her to dinner so she wouldn't be alone this evening. Pulling out her phone, she dialed her friend from church.

Joan was excited to hear from her. "I'd love to do dinner with you, Mads! In fact, I've got some chicken wings and a pizza being delivered. We can eat up here or at your place. Which would you prefer?"

"Your place. Mine is still a work in progress."

"Come on up any time, then."

Delighted, Maddie got ready to go up to Joan's. Just as she reached her door, someone started banging on it. Maddie froze.

"Open up, Maddie! I know you're in there!" It was Joe!

Maddie backed away from the door, glad she had locked it when she entered. What should she do? Call the police? Janie? Joan? Rick? She couldn't justify the police to herself; after all, he hadn't done anything to her. Yet. And what could Janie or Joan do? Not much except argue with him. What about Rick? He was muscular enough to stand up to Joe, but. . .

"Maddie!" bellowed Joe, rattling the door handle. "Let me in! I just want to talk to you!"

Shaking, she flipped her phone open and dialed her father. "Dad, Joe's here at my door! I'm scared!" she told him. "Can you come over? You know where Joan lives. I'm in apartment 2B."

"Be right there!"

Maddie backed into the kitchen and sat down. Quietly she called Joan and told her she'd be delayed and to go ahead without her. She closed the phone before Joan could ask any questions. Joe continued to pound on the door, pleading with Maddie to open up and let him in.

"I've changed, Maddie," he said reassuringly. But Maddie refused to answer him, just sat still as a mouse and waited for her father to come. Nearly ten minutes later, Maddie heard her father's voice outside her door talking with Joe.

"You need to leave, Joe," she heard her father say. "You're not part of Maddie's life anymore."

"But I want to be! She's my wife!"

"Ex-wife," corrected the pastor. "Come on, now, let's move out of the hallway. We're disturbing all the tenants."

"No! I'm not leaving until I talk with Maddie!"

Maddie was about to go and open the door and face Joe when she heard sirens approaching. She figured one of her neighbors had called the police. Joe, Roper, and Gene Halverson, a friend Roper had brought with him, heard the sirens also. Joe glared at the two men who shook their heads. Then the front door at the bottom of the stairs opened and four police bounded up the stairs, hands ready to reach for their guns if necessary. Joe's eyes blazed with fury.

"I didn't do anything wrong!" he yelled at them. "I was just trying to see my wife but she won't let me in."

"Ex-wife," said Roper automatically. "There's also a restraining order out on him," he explained to the police. Joe's head whipped toward him and he took a threatening step forward. The two closest police grabbed his arms but he threw them off easily.

"Sir," said the burliest officer, getting in his face, "we could arrest you for attempted assault. If you don't want that, then I suggest you get control of your temper, back off from trying to see your ex-wife, and leave the premises immediately. Peacefully. Leave or get arrested," he said, standing directly in front of Skeeter, blocking Maddie's door.

Skeeter was breathing heavily, seething with anger, but he knew he was outnumbered and raised his hands halfway in surrender. He backed toward the stairs, glaring at Roper as he passed him, then turned and hurried down. Three policemen followed him, two grabbing his arms and escorting him outside. The fourth one knocked on Maddie's door and identified herself. Maddie opened the door and invited everyone in so they could talk in private.

"How long has your ex-husband been stalking you, ma'am?" asked Officer Shirley Perkins.

"He just showed up this afternoon where I work, then here tonight. I haven't seen him since I left him eighteen months ago. I don't know how he found out where I was."

The officer encouraged Maddie to fill her in on the reason for the divorce and responded sympathetically to her. "If he shows up again to harass you or stalk you anywhere, anytime, call us. We don't like guys who beat up their wives. What I'm going to do is write up a report on this so there's a file on Mr. Skeeter. Do be on your guard constantly. Stay near friends. Don't go out alone. You know, standard precautions." Perkins stood then, shook everyone's hands, and departed.

Roper looked at his daughter trying not to show how worried he was. "Come back home, Mads," he said.

"No, Dad. I need to be able to stand on my own two feet. I'm sorry I had to call you tonight, but I was stuck in here and I didn't know who else to call. Thank you, and you, too, Gene, for coming over here. I'll be alright now." She plastered a smile on her face to convince them but her father didn't buy it. However, he didn't say anything, he just gave her a long, hard hug. Halverson shook her hand and told her to call him any time Skeeter came around. He knew how to handle jerks like him!

They left and Maddie wilted onto her couch, grateful the excitement was over.

Ten minutes later, a gentle knock sounded at the door. At first startled, Maddie quickly realized that Joe didn't know how to knock gently, so she got up and went to see who was there. It was her neighbor from across the hall.

"Come in," said Maddie. "Were you my guardian angel tonight who called the police?"

"Yes," the woman answered. "Hi, my name is Robin Hastings. I was so worried about you. I peeked out and saw what a big man he was and I was afraid he'd break down your door. So I called the cops."

"Thank you so much!" said Maddie earnestly, squeezing the woman's hands. "I was so relieved when they came! My name is Maddie Roper. I'm delighted to meet you, Robin."

When Robin left, Maddie went into her kitchen to find something to eat. Not that she was very hungry now. Her stomach was upset again but she needed to put something in it. Just then, another gentle knock sounded at her door. Thinking it was Robin Hastings again, she hurried over to open it. Instead, there stood Joan with a plate of food, smiling uncertainly at her.

"Come in!"

"I didn't know what was going on down here but I heard the commotion and the sirens and police, so when you didn't come up to my apartment, I decided to bring the pizza and wings down here. Have you eaten yet?"

"No, I sure haven't. Joanie, you're a gem!" Maddie led her into the kitchen and when Joan uncovered the plate of food, Maddie's mouth immediately started watering. Her stomachache disappeared.

"They're not very hot anymore, although I did put them in the oven to stay warm in case you were able to come up to eat. What happened? I could hear the yelling all the way to the end of the hall."

"Remember I told you about Joe, my ex? Well, he showed up at work and then here tonight," explained Maddie between bites of pizza, "He wouldn't go away so I called my father and he and Gene Halverson came over to reason with Joe."

"Which did no good, I gather, since the police came."

"Yeah, my neighbor, Robin Hastings, called them.

"Do you want to talk about Joe, Mads? I don't know many details about why you two divorced, though I heard through the church grapevine that you lost your baby."

So Maddie told Joan the whole story. Joan teared up as she listened.

"I'm so sorry," whispered Joan. "I had no idea it had been that bad." She squeezed Maddie's hands and Maddie made her promise not to spread the information around the church.

That night Maddie had trouble sleeping. Memories invaded her dreams and she woke up several times. In the morning she felt headachy and debated about taking the day off, but decided she needed to go in and at least check in with Rick how the Berman hearing went.

He came to her office as soon as she arrived, eager to relate his experience in court. He gave her a verbatim account; she could picture everyone talking and the actions of the judge. "It was fantastic!" he ended.

"I'm glad you enjoyed yourself so much. Thankfully, the Bermans are an easy case, without a lot of contention. It was good preparation at least to wet your feet."

"Thanks," he said. "Now I need to talk to you about Roger. Did Janie tell you about me switching over to him so I can take over some of his cases when he leaves?"

"Yup. He's a good guy, you'll like him. He does things a little differently than I do, but then I guess we all develop our own style."

"I'm going to miss working with you, Maddie," he told her. "You have a great style with your clients and most of them appreciate it.

"Thanks, Rick," she said, grinning. How different from Joe he was! How could her parents not like him?

"That brings me up to tonight. Are we still on for dinner?"

"Yes, we are. I'm settled in the apartment and although I had a very rough evening last night, I'd like to go out to dinner with you. However, I'm going to leave early today and take a nap before we go out. Do you want me to meet you at a certain restaurant?"

"No, I'll pick you up, say 6:30? I was thinking of a nice seafood restaurant. Is that okay with you?"

"Perfect."

"What was rough about last night? Your stomach still bothering you?"

"Yes, and it was caused by an unwanted visitor who came here yesterday afternoon and upset me and then again last night at my apartment. I never expected to see my ex-husband again, but there he was."

"What happened last night?"

Maddie told him and watched as Rick gritted his teeth and frowned. He was grateful Roper and Halverson went over there and that a neighbor had called the police, but he would have liked to have been there to protect her himself.

"Maddie," he said quietly, "please call me if he shows up again to harass you, ever. I want to be there! Let me give you my cell number." He dictated his number while she plugged it into her cell.

"Thank you, Rick. Now I've got you, Dad, Gene, Janie, Marcia, the police, my neighbor Robin, and my good friend Joan all watching out for me. I feel so much safer than I did yesterday! You guys are all wonderful!"

"We do our best," he said and stood up. "I've got to report to Roger in a few minutes. I'll see you at 6:30 tonight. Where something nice, okay?"

She nodded and watched him leave. What a great guy he was turning out to be! She was glad he was on her team and she wished now she had called him last night as well as her father. If Joe showed up again, she decided she would call Rick and Gene first.

Somehow she made it through her day without any further incidents with Joe showing up, but she feared he'd be watching and waiting for her every time she left her apartment or CPS and found herself getting anxious about how to deal with him by herself. Then she remembered Officer Shirley Perkin's comment to call her if he tried anything like that, and Rick's and Gene's comments to the same effect, and she felt better.

CHAPTER 7

The Abandoned Baby

MADDIE WAS READY BEFORE Rick arrived that evening. She was surprised at how excited she was to be going out on a real date. Debating which outfit to wear, since he said wear something nice, she ultimately chose a light green dress which brought out the green in her eyes. Checking herself in the mirror she hoped she looked attractive and perky for him.

But, what would they talk about? He knew her story now about Joe but, she thought, she knew very little about his short marriage to Betty or his family and childhood. She didn't want to talk about work and cases, that was for sure, nor his transferring over to work with Roger. So, what was left? The weather? Of course, that was always a good topic of conversation in Colorado close to the mountains. She was still mulling that over when a knock on her door at 6:30 on the dot cut her musings short. She opened it to find Rick standing there, a dimpled grin on his face and a bouquet of flowers in his hand.

"A house-warming gift," he explained as she accepted the flowers and went in search of a vase for them.

"Thank you! They're beautiful!"

"I like what you chose to wear. It matches your eyes," commented Rick. He walked around the apartment, nodding and smiling. "You've done a great job getting your place in order, Maddie. It feels homey and comfortable. I like it. I like your choice in furniture, too."

Maddie chuckled since he'd helped pick it out. She joined him in the living room and thanked him for the compliment on her dress and her apartment, coat and gloves in hand. Rick helped her on with her coat and they headed out into a fairly comfortable evening for Colorado Springs in November. In the car, Maddie asked which restaurant they were going to and he told her the Bonefish Grill.

"Love that place!" she enthused. "You ever been there before, Rick?"

"No, but I asked around and everyone recommended it, so that's why we're going there."

After they were seated and their orders taken, Rick said apologetically, "I need to ask you one work-related question and tell you about working with Roger. Do you mind? After that, shoptalk is off limits."

"Deal. What's your question?"

"How do I deal with a clingy client? One of Roger's female clients was so relieved when I showed up that she totally ignored him and wanted to deal only with me. I mean," he said laughing self-consciously, "I'm used to women throwing themselves at me because of my charm and good looks, but this was different." Turning serious, he asked, "What's the best way to deal with that? What if she were my client and I was alone with her, no Roger or you with me to intervene?"

"It's not uncommon," answered Maddie dead-pan, "for someone with your charm and good looks to have this problem." Rick just rolled his eyes.

"You're not helping," he said.

"Sorry," she said grinning, "I couldn't resist. Seriously, I can think of two things you could do. One is to remain professional and by that I mean do not respond to that kind of behavior. Forget you're a man; pretend you're a rock. That's how other guys have handled it, from what I hear. Also, if she's the touchy-feely kind of person and puts her hand on your arm or, especially, your leg, gently but firmly remove her hand from your body and carry on as if she hadn't done anything. You don't have to be cold about it, but definitely make it clear that you don't want that. The other thing you could do is keep her talking, keep her mind on the business at hand. Get her mentally involved in solving her parental problems so she can get her children back. She may be as needy a person as her children are, starved for love and attention, but it's not your job to satisfy her needs. You're there for the children and to help her get them back. You might even need to arrange an appointment with a therapist to help her deal with her needs and her lack of boundaries." Maddie took a breath. "Did that answer your question?"

"Yes, that makes a lot of sense. Thanks. Now, just a comment about going out with Roger. His style was so different from yours I kept wanting to take over and do things your way. I had to keep biting my tongue to stop myself."

"Well, when you have his cases, you'll get to work them your own way, if that's any consolation."

Rick nodded. "Yeah. In other words, I have to develop my own style." Maddie nodded.

Their food arrived a moment later and conversation virtually stopped while they devoured the delicious morsels on their plates. The rest of the dinner, dessert and decaf coffee went smoothly. They chatted about everything. Maddie learned a little more about Rick, his parents, his siblings, his childhood, his time in the Army, and his wife. Maddie talked about growing up a "PK," a preacher's kid.

"I was so bad!" she told him laughing. "I got in trouble at school, at church, in the neighborhood, everywhere! My parents didn't know what to do with me."

"I find that impossible to believe!" commented Rick truthfully.

"Believe it. You can even ask my parents. They'll also tell you I brought home every stray animal—or human—I found. That's how Joe entered my life. I was trying to help him. First, it was to study so he'd be able to graduate. Then it was to find a job. Then, in Pueblo, it was to find another job. He always needed help with something. But let's not get into that right now. This has been a wonderful evening and I don't want to mar it with my troubles with Joe."

"No sign of him today?" Rick asked quietly, watching her closely.

"No, thank goodness. Can we talk about something else?"

"Sure. Anything you'd like."

Leaving the restaurant later, Rick drove them to a nearby park and they got out and walked, holding hands. They chatted about church things and members he'd met, one of whom was Gene Halverson, Maddie's youth group and what he himself could get involved in. He thought he might like to join the choir so Maddie told him they met at 7:00 Wednesday evenings for rehearsal. He agreed to come next week and check it out. When they realized they were getting chilled, Rick took Maddie home and kissed her goodnight at her door.

Maddie smiled to herself. What a pleasant night, she thought. And the kiss. Not a hungry kiss or a French kiss or a demanding kiss like Joe's. Just sweet and light. A perfect kiss for a first date. Rick, heading for his car whistled a happy tune. The night had gone perfectly for him.

Sunday morning, Maddie got to church early so she could grab a sweet roll. As she got out of her car and headed for the front door she noticed a lumpy blanket off to one side, laying on the lawn. She approached it, getting more and more concerned.

The "lump" inside the blanket was moving! She stooped down and gingerly pulled the blanket back to see what was inside.

It was a baby! A newborn baby, kicking it's little legs and crying, face all scrunched up! Maddie gently rewrapped the baby and lifted it and the blanket up and carried it into the church. Joan saw her and came over.

"What have you got there?" she asked cheerfully.

"A baby," whispered Maddie.

"A baby! Maddie, I didn't even know you were pregnant!" laughed Joan, teasingly.

Maddie shot her a look. "It's not mine. It was lying out by the front door." Several other people came over to see what Maddie was holding. When they realized it was a baby, they led her into the nursery and she laid the baby down in one of the cribs, gently pulling the blanket off.

"It's a little brown girl," whispered Joan. "Mexican? A black-white mix?"

"Whose is it?" asked several people. Maddie explained about finding the baby outside to the group that had assembled in the nursery with her.

"I need to call Child Protective Services," she commented and left the baby to be watched by the dozen or so people who had crammed into the small room. She went out in the hall and dialed Janie and told her the news. "It's a little girl and she was left with no bottle, diapers, clothes, or anything else."

"I'll send someone over right away, Maddie, including the police. "Does she seem to be okay?"

"Yes, except she has a weak cry and is probably cold and very hungry."

No Sunday school classes met that morning as CPS workers and the police arrived and took over. One CPS worker bundled up the baby and took her to the emergency shelter until a foster home could be found for her. A second worker and the police questioned everyone about when the baby arrived, if they had seen the person dropping the baby off, etc. After the worker and police left, it was all everybody talked about.

Pastor Roper did his best to gather and quiet the people down before the worship service but people had a hard time concentrating or sitting still. This was more excitement than their little church had ever seen.

"Quite an exciting time for the people this morning," commented Roper to Maddie afterwards. "I missed it all, unfortunately, but I heard all about it. I'm going to have to start coming to church earlier," he joked.

Lucy Roper joined them as the last of the members departed, Lucy barely looking Maddie in the eyes and not looking at Rick at all. He felt bad about that; he wished he'd never gone to dinner over there last Sunday and caused her so much distress.

"It's good to see you again, Mrs. Roper," he said, hoping if he acted like everything was alright it would be. She turned to him and saw the smile on his face.

Bracing herself, she asked, "How are you?"

"Just fine," he assured her. "You look pretty in that outfit," he complimented her, trying to distract her. Surprised, Lucy looked down at her lilac pants suit, then back up and smiled her thanks.

"Gary always liked this on me, so I wear it a lot."

"Very becoming," said Rick. Turning to Roper, he said, "I enjoyed your sermon about counting our blessings, sir. Sometimes we need reminding to do that." Beaming, Roper shook his hand and thanked him.

Then, with a twinkle in his eye, he asked, "Do we dare try another Sunday dinner together? We're having roast beef today."

Rick glanced at Maddie and saw her nod so he accepted. He wasn't sure if the Ropers were just trying to make up for the grilling last week and the awkwardness at the end or if they were genuinely wanting to just have a nice meal together. Well, he'd soon find out.

The dinner went smoothly. Lucy barely spoke but she listened attentively. Roper and Maddie did most of the talking, a lot of it about the baby and what the procedure was to take care of it. Rick listened and took it all in, grateful the attention wasn't on him this time.

"She'll go into a foster home right away because the shelter isn't equipped to care for infants that young and, if no one comes forward to claim her, she'll eventually be put up for adoption."

"Have you had babies dropped on your doorstep before?" asked Rick.

"Not mine personally," laughed Maddie, "but babies have been taken to the fire department and the police who then brought them to CPS. Our adoptions are contracted out to an agency who finds a family for them."

"I bet the foster parents hate to give them up."

"Many are fost-adopt homes, meaning they have first dibs on adopting the baby."

"We should have adopted children when you were young," commented Lucy. "Then you'd have had brothers and sisters to play with."

"Nah. I loved being an only child. I got all the attention!" She grinned good-naturedly at her mother who smiled back at her and chuckled.

"Is, uh, is it alright if I say you were a handful?" she asked sheepishly.

Maddie laughed outright. "It's okay, I already told Rick what a little hellion I was."

The conversation bantered back and forth then with the Ropers asking Rick questions about his family. He cheerfully told them he'd been a brat too but had finally settled down when he went into the Army. They learned about his aborted marriage, getting his degree, and seeking work at CPS. Altogether, it was a much more enjoyable afternoon for him than the previous Sunday.

At work the next morning, everyone was buzzing about the baby, whom they affectionately named Susie Q. A foster home had been found for her right away and the foster mom, Doris Wheaton, brought her into the office. Having been fed and dressed warmly, she was a much happier baby than the day before. They guessed she was barely two days old, probably born sometime on Saturday. Doris, a cheerful, young housewife married to an up-and-coming CPA, told them they already knew they were going to adopt Susie Q if no one came forward to claim her.

Everyone eventually wandered back to their offices or out to court and home visits. Work had to go on. Doris left with Susie Q and Maddie headed for the Durants first to see how the weekend visit with Dawn went. Mimi invited her in, full of smiles.

"I had a wonderful visit with Dawn," she announced happily. "She looks well, is happy she'll be moving to a foster home this week, but couldn't stop talking and crying about what Ollie did to her. I just listened. She knew she made a mistake getting in his car, but what happened afterwards was entirely his fault, not hers, and I told her so. No one asks to get raped! I just pray she doesn't get pregnant. We'll know if she misses her next period. Maddie, will she be able to get an abortion since she was raped?"

"Yes, it's legal here in Colorado and public funds are even provided in the instance of rape. There are clinics, hospitals and doctors who can provide the service, if that's what you really want to do."

"I can't imagine Fred putting up with Dawn getting more and more pregnant-looking. I think it's best to get rid of the baby so we can get on with life and put this behind us." Maddie kept silent but she was concerned about Mimi's apparently cavalier attitude toward "getting rid of the baby."

"Mimi, Dawn will need professional counseling if she decides to get an abortion. In fact, I think it's required by law. Getting raped is a traumatic experience and then, if she aborts the baby as well, it will only add to her distress. Think this through carefully. Carrying the baby to term and putting it up for adoption is another alternative. Many people out there can't have children and one of them would love to adopt Dawn's baby. In fact," she added, "we just had a baby dropped off at church yesterday morning which will probably be put up for adoption. Were you at church yesterday?"

"No. Fred didn't want to go. What happened? Tell me about the baby." So Maddie filled her in and was encouraged by the look of possibility in Mimi's eyes regarding Dawn carrying the baby to term and putting it up for adoption.

The rest of the day sped along. She got all her visits in and her one court hearing and was on her way back to CPS when she noticed what looked like Joe's black Silverado behind her. Her stomach lurched. Was it him? She couldn't quite tell. Two blocks later, it turned right onto a cross street and she breathed a sigh of relief. Going home that night, she again thought she saw the Silverado. It followed her for a few blocks before veering off. Shakily, she went on home.

CHAPTER 8

Stalker

TUESDAY, IT HAPPENED AGAIN. The truck showed up on her tail each time she drove away from CPS or a home visit or the court and then would veer off. On the way home that night, however, it stayed behind her all the way to her apartment. She saw it start to pull into a vacant parking spot near her building, so she stepped on the gas and drove quickly past her parking slot and headed for the parsonage. Scared, heart beating rapidly, she prayed he wouldn't come there and cause trouble for her parents. When she saw Joe come up behind her, she stepped on the gas to get to her parents more quickly. Once there, she wasted no time and hurried in, apologizing for not calling them first and, with words tumbling out faster than she ever talked, she explained the situation. As expected, her parents became alarmed and anxious.

"You call Rick, Mads, and I'll call Gene Halverson. Joe won't try anything if we have reinforcements here."

Maddie quickly explained the situation to Rick and he said he'd be right over. Halverson said he'd be right over too. Both arrived within minutes.

"Is there a black Silverado out there?" asked Roper. Both men nodded.

"I suggest we turn out the lights in the living room and go in the kitchen," suggested Halverson. "Are your doors and windows all locked?" Roper scurried around double checking everything. Then they turned out the lights and withdrew to the kitchen.

"Have any of you eaten?" asked Lucy. Everyone looked at her, surprised she could think of food at a time like this, but dutifully shook their heads no. "Good. We were just about to eat and I've got a chicken casserole in the oven big enough for an army."

As they ate, they had Maddie tell them in detail about Joe's surveillance of her the last couple of days.

"I'm afraid I'm endangering my clients with him following me to their homes and I'm afraid to go home and be grabbed by him before I can get into my apartment and lock him out. But I can't keep running to you, Dad, every time he shows up."

Rick sat and listened. He had a solution in mind but hesitated bringing it up.

"Move back home, Mads," said Lucy. "Then Dad can protect you better."

"No, Mom. I'll only be endangering the two of you."

"You're supposed to call that policewoman, aren't you, if he comes around?" asked Lucy. "Well, it seems clear to me that Joe is stalking you, so I think you should contact her and let her know."

"I forgot about her," admitted Maddie.

A silence followed and Rick decided to voice his suggestion. "I've got an idea," he said. "I think I can protect Maddie from Joe—if I'm there at her apartment with her." He paused, waiting for their reaction but they just sat and waited for him to say more. "If I transported Maddie to and from work and stayed with her in the apartment, I could stop him from hurting her."

"Oh, Rick, I can't ask you to do that!," responded Maddie. "For one thing, I need my own car so I can go see my clients during the day. You can't take me around since you have your own cases now. And my apartment's so small, we'd be cramped."

"Okay, we'll drive two cars but your apartment is big enough to sleep two people. You have a great couch I can sleep on."

Maddie stared at him, realizing he meant it. Pros: he was pretty big and strong and might be able to handle Joe; also he was pleasant to be around; and it would be fun to cook for two. Cons: she didn't want the two men fighting over her; Rick was way too desirable to be close to; and she wasn't really ready for domestic life yet, even for only a few days.

Rick was watching her as the emotions played across her face, reading her thoughts clearly.

"I promise to be a gentleman at all times," he went on doggedly. "I'm good at picking up after myself, I can make a mean batch of scrambled eggs and great grilled cheese sandwiches. Besides, hopefully this will only be for a few days until he gets the message to butt out of your life." He gave her a reassuring smile. He didn't dare look at her parents.

"Joe's a big guy, bigger than you" cautioned Roper. "And more muscular. He scares me, frankly. When we went to Mads' apartment, I stood up to him, but as a pastor, certainly not as his equal physically."

"I'm Army-conditioned and trained," Rick told him. "I work out regularly and I scale mountains for fun. I can handle guys bigger than myself, sir. I just want to protect Maddie."

Roper looked at his daughter who nodded affirmatively. Reassured, he said, "Rick has my vote. Plus that policewoman. Why don't we give it a try for a few days, okay?" he asked, looking at Lucy.

"Do I have a say in this?" she asked.

"Sure, Mom, of course."

"Well, I don't like it! Nothing against you personally, Rick, but Maddie," she said, addressing her daughter directly, "you've only known Rick a very short while and he may be everything he says he is, but you don't know that for sure. You're too trusting, Mads. You trusted Joe and look what happened. I'd rather Dad went over and stayed with you."

"No, Lucy," answered Roper quickly. "I'm not up to that. Joe was not a reasonable man to deal with the other night. Mads needs someone younger, stronger, and more capable. I think Rick will do just fine. He's offered his services and I think we should accept."

"Mrs. Roper, I promise I will do everything in my power to protect Maddie. I think I can handle Joe. I won't do anything to hurt Maddie. I don't take advantage of women. I was brought up to protect and care for them. I promise you, Maddie will be safe with me. However," he said, pausing, "if Maddie would rather get someone else, I'll understand. It was just a thought."

"Mom, I'm willing to give it a try. I trust Rick. He's been a complete gentleman to me since the day we met. I'd like to give it a shot."

Lucy sat back in her chair, lips pursed. "Well, I guess it's decided then!" she snapped. "You are so damn trusting! You think everyone's a perfect angel, just misunderstood. And then you find out the hard way that they're no angel at all. Like Joe. You're just not discriminating enough!"

Maddie's mouth dropped open at her mother's curse and sharp tone of voice.

Gene Halverson had sat quietly throughout the whole exchange and got up now and went over to Lucy's chair, putting his hands on her shoulders, gently massaging them. "Relax, Lucy," he said quietly. "I've come to know Rick at church; we've had several conversation and I find him to be a well-grounded, fine, upstanding, moral young man. He's strong and capable, ethical, and has only Maddie's welfare at heart. He has my vote of confidence. But if it will make you feel any better, Lucy, I'll keep an eye on the two of them since I live just around the corner from

Maddie's apartment building." Over the top of Lucy's head, he winked at Maddie and Rick and they both relaxed.

Lucy stood up without a word and walked out of the room. Maddie looked at her father.

"I'll take care of your mother," he said. "Why don't you take advantage of this time to leave and get yourselves settled in your apartment. And Rick," he said turning to him. "I agree with Gene in his assessment of you, but please, don't let me down. Maddie is precious to us."

"No, sir, I won't. I promise you." Roper nodded and walked the two of them to the door. "Joe is really an awful person," he said, "and strong as an ox. Be very careful."

"Yes, sir, I will."

Outside, Rick told Maddie to follow him to his apartment while he got some clothes and toiletries, then they'd go to her apartment and get settled. Maddie nodded and got in her car. Both noticed that the Silverado was gone and sighed with relief. They drove in tandem to Rick's apartment and Maddie went up with him at his request. His apartment was bigger than hers, but it was basically a bachelor pad, sparsely furnished. Watching for the Silverado, Maddie led the way to her apartment where they found the Silverado waiting for them. Maddie sat in her car until Rick came over. He immediately took her hand and hurried her up the stairs to her apartment, securely locking the door once they were safely inside. They stood in the dark and listened at the door for Joe's footsteps on the stairs, but all was quiet.

Just as they started to relax, however, heavy footsteps pounded up toward the apartment. Rick pushed Maddie behind him, whispering for her to close herself in the bedroom. Then the pounding began on the door and Skeeter started hollering for Maddie to open up. He continued pounding until he heard sirens blaring and flashing lights penetrating the window in the downstairs' door. Rick held his peace throughout, watching and waiting. Joe's barrage on the door ended and he hustled up the stairs to the next floor.

In another moment, a different knock sounded at the door.

"Police! Open up!"

Rick quickly unlocked the door and Maddie came out from the bedroom. Officer Shirley Perkins, who had interviewed Maddie at Joe's previous visit, and another officer Maddie hadn't seen before stood there looking expectant.

"Where is he?" asked Perkins.

"He ran upstairs," answered Rick. Perkins sent her partner up to search for Skeeter and came into the apartment. She got the story from them and scowled at Maddie.

"I told you to call me if he came around, Ms. Roper," she chided.

"But he only pestered me, following me in the car and then veering off. He hadn't broken any laws."

"Yes, he had. Tailing you around like that is called stalking, ma'am, and it is definitely breaking the law, especially with a restraining order in place."

Maddie bowed her head. "I didn't want to awfulize it and aggravate him by calling the police," she admitted.

Perkin's look softened. "You are obviously a very sweet, loving woman, which means you're not a match for a nut like Skeeter." Rick explained to her that he would be staying with Maddie for a few days to protect her.

Perkins' partner, Officer Donell Thornapple, returned from his search for Skeeter. "The guy's long gone. He made it to the roof and somehow managed to disappear. Sorry."

Perkins finished her report, then thanked Rick for staying with Maddie. She made them both promise to call the very next time Skeeter showed his face.

"If all you see is Skeeter's nose, you call me! If you only see his foot, you call me! If you see that black Silverado, you definitely call me, ASAP! Got it, Maddie?"

"Got it," she answered meekly. Rick nodded more assertively, assuring Perkins he would make sure the call got made.

Somehow that evening, Maddie and Rick got themselves organized enough in her apartment to make it to their separate beds at a decent time.

But Maddie lay in her bed for a long time without sleeping. Her anxiety about Joe and the situation she was in wormed around in her brain and when she did doze off, it invaded her dreams. At 4:00, she was wide awake again but she didn't want to wander out of the bedroom for fear of disturbing Rick. She was very aware of his nearness and of wanting him to hold her in his strong arms and make her feel safe. She wanted his comfort. In fact, to her utter surprise, she wanted him, and heat flooded her body. Ashamed of her sexual desire at a time like this, she sat on the side of the bed and tried to stop thinking about him.

Not knowing what else to do, she forcibly turned her thoughts to Joe. Why had he shown up all of a sudden after eighteen months? Where had he been during all that time? What had he been doing? Was he still drinking? Was he still obsessed with her? Well, that answer was clear enough: he was. He was picking up right where he left off. Although part of her still cared about Joe she didn't want to be around him ever again. His showing up here and tailing her everywhere made her fear things would go from bad to worse. Feeling trapped and scared, she sobbed quietly.

Then, bowing her head in prayer, she prayed for much needed guidance about what to do about Joe. As she'd done many times in the past, she pictured herself in her quiet place with Jesus standing by her side, gently resting a hand on her shoulder. Gradually, she felt the warmth of God's love surrounding her, the strength she needed invigorating her, the certitude of God's loving presence relaxing her, and was surprised when she next opened her eyes to find herself lying on her side in bed with sunlight streaming brightly in through her bedroom window.

She rose quietly and headed for the shower, wondering how Rick slept and what this new day would bring. She also wondered if he really did know how to make a mean batch of scrambled eggs; her stomach was growling.

He did, and she raved over them.

By Friday, they had settled into a workable routine. Both were early risers and every morning, Rick cooked up his tasty batch of scrambled eggs. Maddie finally suggested she make breakfast just to have a change from the eggs. Laughing, he turned the kitchen back over to her.

Maddie relaxed more and more each day. She hadn't seen Joe or his Silverado since Tuesday and was hoping and praying he would just disappear and never come back to bother her again. In the meantime, she was finding out Rick was every bit the gentleman he claimed to be. He treated her like a favorite sister, which, for the moment at least, was fine with her. And, always, he hovered discreetly and protectively about her outside of work as he'd promised. She felt so safe with him.

That evening, Rick suggested they go out to eat. The danger from Joe seemed to be past and Rick felt they could venture out more in public. He took her to an Italian restaurant where Maddie enjoyed her manicotti and a small glass of wine and was more relaxed and like her old self again. Rick was encouraged and relaxed, too. Consequently, he wasn't paying near enough attention as they left the restaurant.

CHAPTER 9

Confrontation

AS SOON AS THEY walked out the door, a dark shadow immediately separated itself from the side of the building and grabbed Rick by his coat collar and swung him around, slamming his back into the brick wall. Momentarily stunned, Rick quickly recovered and snapped his arms up to break Skeeter's hold on him, barely succeeding. Skeeter responded with a wild punch to Rick's face. Fortunately, Rick saw it coming and easily dodged it, roughly pushing the man away from him.

"What the hell are you doing with my woman?" Skeeter demanded, glaring malevolently.

"Keep your voice down!" ordered Rick. "Let's move away from the building. No need putting on a show for the customers." He backed away from Skeeter, grabbing Maddie's hand in the process and pulling her with him. Turning briskly, he hurried them over to his car, his nerves jangling with adrenalin. He expected Skeeter to grab him from behind but, as luck would have it, Skeeter was caught off guard by Rick's take-charge attitude and hesitated just long enough for them to be able to reach Rick's car. Skeeter's face hardened, though, when he saw Rick holding Maddie's hand and rage fueled him. He lurched forward to catch up with them.

"Hey!" he yelled. But Rick and Maddie ignored him. As soon as they reached his car, he told her to get inside. Her heart thumping with fear for Rick, she did as she was told. She watched as he turned to face Skeeter coming up swiftly. When Skeeter stopped, his face red with rage, Rick was ready, projecting a calmness he didn't feel, legs apart for balance, a steely look in his eyes. They stood there, waiting to see who would make the first move.

"What the hell do you think you're doing with my wife?" Skeeter demanded.

"First of all, you're divorced, Skeeter, so she's not your wife anymore," answered Rick. Skeeter raised his arm menacingly, then threw a punch at Rick's face, but Rick saw it coming and easily sidestepped it. The punch landed on the car. Skeeter yelped.

"Stop!" said Rick in his Army Lieutenant voice. Joe looked at him in surprise. "Listen to me, Skeeter! Everything you've been doing this past week is going to get you in trouble with the law. Stalking is a crime, a felony violation. So is violating a protective order. Besides that, you're scaring the daylights out of Maddie. Is that want you want to do? Do you really think scaring her to death is going to make her want to return to you? Are you nuts, man?"

Skeeter glared at Rick but said nothing.

"I know your history, Skeeter, that you've hurt Maddie in the past, that you beat her up so bad you caused her to lose your baby. She left you to preserve her health. And I know that you know what you're doing now is wrong, because when the police came, you ran away."

Joe's face crumbled. "Baby?"

"That's right. You kicked her in the stomach and she lost the baby. You knew she was pregnant; she told you."

"When? I don't remember that."

"The night you came home smashed. She told you about the baby but you started beating her and then kicking her repeatedly in the stomach!" Rick dared him to deny it.

"I. . .I don't remember that," stammered Skeeter. "All I remember is passing out and waking up and Maddie was gone."

"You had a black out."

"I guess." The fight seemed to have gone out of him. "She was pregnant? For real?" he asked unbelievingly.

"For real. But not for long. She hemorrhaged from being kicked viciously in the stomach and had to be rushed to the hospital. You killed your baby, Skeeter!"

Skeeter looked in the car at Maddie, subdued, anguish temporarily clouding the anger in his eyes. "Can I talk to her for a moment? I haven't had a drink in months. I'm clean." Rick nodded cautiously and let Skeeter go around to Maddie's side of the car but followed close behind him.

"Maddie? Can you roll the window down so I can talk to you?" Rick shook his head no so she kept it closed. "Please," pleaded Skeeter, his face close to Maddie's window. "I love you! I want a second chance! I've been dry for over a year now. I won't ever hit you again, I promise. Please, come back and live with me."

Maddie shook her head no vigorously and Skeeter raised his hands to the window. Maddie scooted as far away from him as she could get. Rick grabbed Skeeter's arm, who turned and knocked it away. A hateful look had returned to his eyes.

"Back off, you punk!" he growled at Rick.

Rick turned and quickly hurried into the driver's side of the car, slammed the locks down, started the car, and pulled away leaving Skeeter standing there staring after them open mouthed. Rick drove several blocks, pulled into another parking lot, slid in between two parked cars, and doused his lights. A few minutes later, they saw the Silverado drive slowly past searching for them. When it kept on going, they both let out the breath they'd been holding. Rick waited another few minutes, then turned to Maddie.

"I suggest we go to my place tonight because I have no doubt he'll go to yours and wait for us. Maddie nodded her okay and he pulled out of the parking lot and headed in the opposite direction from Skeeter. Rick wound in and around various streets in case Skeeter had spotted his car and was following. Finally, they arrived at his apartment. When he ascertained that there was no sign of Skeeter, he hurried Maddie into his building and up the elevator to his apartment.

Inside, Maddie sat down wearily on his couch and closed her eyes. Rick joined her, taking her hands in his.

"You're safe here, Maddie," he said.

"Oh, Rick, this is turning into a nightmare for you! I've got you involved in something that has nothing to do with you, but now you're on his shit-list, too. But I'm so proud of how you stood up to him! I was so afraid he would hurt you, but you handled him well."

He nodded his thanks. "My only concern now is that he knows my car as well as yours, which means he'll find out where I live and bring trouble here. I propose we contact Officer Perkins in the morning and get some protection for you. The guy has a one tract mind, you. He was surprised about the baby, though."

"I guess he was too drunk to hear what I was saying. But he must have heard me, Rick, because he deliberately kicked me where it would do the most harm to the baby."

"Yeah, I hear you. But it's still possible for him not to remember it afterwards if he had a blackout. I also wonder where he's been for the past eighteen months. He would have guessed you'd come back home to your parents when you left, wouldn't he? If so, he'd have been up here shortly after he realized you were gone. So, where's he been?"

"I thought he'd be right up here, too, but when he didn't show up for several weeks, I figured he gave up on me and let me go."

"I wonder if he was in jail during that time?" mused Rick.

"I don't want to think about him anymore tonight, Rick. I'm so tired."

"Of course. Let me get the bedroom ready for you."

She grabbed his arm. "No, I can sleep on the couch, Rick. All I need is a pillow and a blanket."

"Absolutely not. Come with me." He took her by the hand and led her into the bedroom which, she noticed, was neat as a pin. She sat on the bed, her eyes already drooping. Rick tossed her a tee-shirt to wear in case she wanted to get out of her good clothes, then quietly gathered a blanket and pillow for himself and left the room. Except for kicking her shoes off, Maddie simply crawled under the covers and snuggled down, barely hearing the door close behind Rick.

She slept like a log until a nightmare invaded her dreams, one involving Joe chasing her and her running as fast as she could but not getting away from him. On top of that, she found she was running around in circles and he just kept pace, an ugly sneer on his face. She woke up with a cry of anguish, the dream still vivid in her mind. She looked around the room and became alarmed, thinking Joe had brought her to a strange place and was hiding her.

Rick knocked on the door and opened it. "Are you alright?" he asked with concern. One look at Rick and Maddie realized where she was and that she was safe.

"I just had a horrid dream," she told him apologetically. He sat on the bed beside her and waited for her to tell him about it. "Joe was chasing me," she said. "I couldn't get away from him. I was running around in circles and he was right behind me the whole time, sneering." The explanation barely covered her fear and distress in the dream.

"I'm sorry," said Rick and cautiously put an arm around her shoulders. She didn't object and they sat like that for several minutes.

"What time is it?" she asked.

"Four o'clock. You want some hot tea or a glass of water?"

"No, thanks. Go back to sleep, Rick. I'm alright now."

"Are you able to go back to sleep?"

"Probably not, but I'll just lay here quietly so you can get your beauty rest."

Chuckling a little, he said, "I'm awake. I'll probably work on my computer a bit. Plus, I'm going to make some tea and you're welcome to come out and join me if you want to."

He left and after a moment she followed him out of the bedroom and into the kitchen. It too was as neat as a pin.

"I'm impressed," she commented.

"About what?"

"You're a neatnik."

He laughed. "My mother did her best, but it was ROTC and the Army that drilled neatness and organization into me." He headed for the pantry and teabags, then got down a four-cup measuring cup, filled it with water, and stuck it in the microwave. When he got out creamer and sweeteners, Maddie smiled to herself.

"What?" he asked. "I happen to like my tea sweet and creamy. You can have yours whatever way you like."

"I just take a little sweetener in mine," she told him, sitting at the table. But while she waited, she turned pensive.

"Thinking about Skeeter?" Rick asked as he steeped the tea in the boiling water. She nodded.

"I really wish he had never come looking for me. I expected him to come up here right after I left him. But when so many months went by, then more than a year, I started to relax, to hope. To heal. I had been so excited about the baby, it really hurt to lose it." Maddie felt the tears filling her eyes and Rick noticed and sat down next to her, taking her hands.

"I'm sorry to dump all this garbage on you, Rick. You're such a sweet guy."

"Have some tea. Maybe it'll help," he suggested.

"Do you always rescue damsels in distress?" she asked, trying to lighten up.

"On occasion. Got to keep my halo shined," he answered with his dimpled smile. "Here's your tea, Maddie. It'll warm you up and make you feel better and if you want to talk about Skeeter and the baby, I'm here to listen."

She squeezed his hand gratefully. What a special person he was! "You know the whole story," she told him. "I don't have to keep going over it. His return has just stirred up all my old feelings of fear and sadness. I'm afraid he's going to wear me down."

"We won't let him. You have a great support system, Maddie, remember? You named them all for me the other day—your parents, Janie, friends at church, Officer Perkins, and me. We're all just a phone call away."

"I know and I'm grateful. And I want you to know again how much I really appreciated how well you handled Joe last night. Not many people stand up to him like that. He's a scary person, especially when he's drunk, although he wasn't even drunk last night and he was scary."

"Tell me about him, Maddie. His childhood, his parents, whatever you know about him." So Maddie told him what she knew: his alcoholic father, his manic-depressive mother, multiple moves because his father couldn't keep a job, and anything else she could think of.

"I was so naïve, Rick. I thought if I could just love him enough he wouldn't hurt so bad or need to drink so much. I was so gullible! Here I was, a social worker, and I couldn't even see the signs of how damaged he was! I guess my mother was right about me trusting people too easily."

"I disagree, Maddie. You're trusting, yes, but I don't think you were gullible. The guy really needed help and it's your nature to reach out to people like him. Did you really love the guy, or did you just want to save him?"

She looked into Rick's eyes. "I don't know," she answered. "I cared a lot for him but I guess I thought I could save him just by loving him."

Rick nodded. "I think Skeeter is obsessed with you, very possessive, but it also seems to me that he considers you his lifeline. He thinks he needs you, desperately. But my guess is what he really needs is therapeutic intervention. I think he's mentally ill, maybe impaired from all the drinking. Whichever, he's a dangerous man, to you and to himself."

"I'm scared, Rick," she admitted.

"I'll protect you the best I can, Maddie. I think you should stay here with me for a while. Call your parents and have them box up some clothes and things for you and mail it to my address. I wish you could take a few days off and just lay low."

"What about my cases? I have to make home visits and appear in court."

"Let's talk to Janie and see if one of the assistants can take you. I want someone with you at all times. If I can, I'll accompany you, but it looks like I'm not going to be able to very often anymore."

On Sunday, they attended church and had dinner with the Ropers. They talked about Friday night and the fight, the plan to hole up in Rick's apartment, to have an assistant at CPS accompany Maddie on all her excursions from the office. Roper approved and was grateful to Rick for taking charge of the situation. His confidence in Rick grew, but Lucy fretted and complained, afraid for her daughter. Rick did his best to reassure her and Lucy reluctantly accepted it. With a sigh, Lucy rose to help Maddie gather the few clothes remaining there in her room. Maddie gave her the key to her apartment and asked her to collect several outfits from there since she didn't know how long this arrangement was going to last. When she and Rick were about to leave, the Ropers clung to her, then released her into Rick's care.

On Monday morning, they approached Janie who sensed immediately that something was up, no doubt with her ex-husband, and invited them in. Rick explained about Skeeter showing up at the restaurant, the ensuing fight, and taking Maddie to his apartment for her safety. Janie listened, her anxiety for Maddie growing. When Rick went on to explain that Maddie didn't have her car and needed someone to drive her to her visits and court hearings, Janie instantly assigned Gina Martinez, a husky Mexican-American woman who took no guff from anyone, to be Maddie's driver and bodyguard. She called Gina in and explained the situation.

"I'd be delighted to protect Maddie!" she said. "Just point the bum out to me when you see him and I'll make sure he doesn't get within a yard of you!" she said to Maddie. Rick couldn't help but smile at Gina's enthusiasm for the job and felt grateful that she was the one Janie chose.

That issue solved, Rick went over to see Roger about the day's agenda and Maddie and Gina went to Maddie's office to discuss their plans for the day. Maddie knew Gina had had a rough marriage and had left her husband several years ago, raising her two children on her own. She'd never finished high school, but after her divorce, she got a job with CPS and went to night school to get her G.E.D. She'd been with the agency over ten years now and she was proud that both her kids went on to college and graduated with honors.

With Gina driving her to her various appointments, it took a while for Skeeter to spot her and begin following. The first time Maddie got out of the car to see some foster kids, Skeeter got out of his car, too, and headed straight for her. He didn't notice Gina jumping out of the driver's seat of her car and approaching him.

"What do you want, mister?" Gina asked him. Startled, Joe turned to her but then dismissed her as just a nosy busybody, and took off after Maddie again. The next thing he knew, he was flat on the sidewalk.

"Hey!" he hollered. "What the hell did you do that for?" He scrambled up and faced Gina.

"Leave the lady alone!" said Gina, glaring at him, hands on her solid hips.

"What the. . .? Who are you?"

"A friend of Maddie's who doesn't want to see her hurt. Go away! Scram!" And she took a threatening step toward him, forcing him to scramble to his feet and back up. Confused by the woman's menacing behavior, Skeeter stood there for a moment debating what to do. He looked toward the door Maddie had gone into then back at Gina.

"Look, she's my wife," he told her in as reasonable a voice as he could muster. "I have every right to see her."

"She's your ex-wife! Now get out of here before I call the cops! You're stalking her and that a very bad thing, mister. Now, scram!" Gina took another step toward Joe and then another. He backed away a few steps then finally turned and headed for his car, fuming with anger. When he looked over at her, she was smirking at him. He drove off full of loathing for the woman, momentarily forgetting all about Maddie.

In the car afterwards, Gina described in detail how she had chased Skeeter off. In gratitude, Maddie took Gina out to lunch and they quickly became fast friends.

The second time that day they found the Silverado tailing them, Gina dropped Maddie off for her home visit, got out of her car and glared at Skeeter as he slowed down to a stop. Her narrowed eyes dared him to tangle with her again. He picked up speed and drove past her.

The third time, he simply drove slowly past them with a vicious, hateful look in his eyes for Gina.

That evening Maddie told Rick about Gina confronting Joe and preventing him from getting close to her. They had a good chuckle at Gina's ingenuity and bravado and both prayed that this arrangement would keep Maddie safe.

"Well, you have a choice for supper tonight," he said, "grilled cheese sandwiches or grilled cheese sandwiches. Which will it be?"

"Let me see what else you have lurking in your frig and then I'll decide," she responded and headed over to find out. "Well," she said after exploring his frig and cupboard, "I could make you a nice tuna casserole with what you've got here, if you'd like, or we could go with your grilled cheese sandwiches." She grinned at him, waiting for his reply.

"Let's save the sandwiches for another night. Tuna casserole sounds mighty good to me right now."

Over dinner they shared stories of their visits that day and Rick said he was learning a lot from Roger but still preferred Maddie's style over Roger's. As for the clingy client he'd told her about, she went and put her hand suggestively on his leg today, but without batting an eye or saying anything, he simply removed it and steered the conversation to the permanency plan they were discussing.

"Then she did it again," he said, "and I removed it the same way. The third time she started to reach over I shook my head no to her and she pulled her hand back. And sulked. She has really pouty lips," he ended, blushing.

Maddie had a good chuckle.

CHAPTER 10

Retaliation

EACH TIME MADDIE AND Gina went out from CPS during the next two days Joe followed them but he never got out of his car. He only parked, watching and waiting, then followed them to their next visit. It was nerve-wracking to the two women, but Maddie felt that as long as he didn't try anything they didn't need to call for help.

Tuesday evening as Gina dropped Maddie off at Rick's, she hugged her and told her to stay close to Rick, she had a bad feeling about this evening. Maddie promised she would and wondered what was worrying Gina.

Unbeknownst to Rick and Maddie, while they were enjoying a quiet evening playing Scrabble, Gina had a quite different evening. She hummed to herself as she drove away from Rick's apartment, happy with her job of protecting Maddie because Maddie was one of her favorite people. She'd assisted her with some of her foster children over the years and thought she was a great social worker. Besides, Maddie always treated her with consideration and respect. Lost in thought, Gina was not aware that Joe was following her home. When she arrived, she headed as usual for her door, keys in hand, but without looking around.

As soon as she got the door open, however, she was shoved from behind into the front hall and fell forward, hitting her nose hard and causing it to bleed. Then her assailant was on top of her, crushing her, and snarling nasty things in her ear. She knew immediately it was Skeeter.

She struggled to get out from under him, but he turned her over forcibly and started punching her in the face. More blood gushed. She sought to gouge out his eyes but he kneeled on her arms, pinning her to the floor while he continued to beat her and then put his hands around her neck and squeezed. Fighting with all her might got her nowhere. She continued to kick and flail, but the tightness in her chest was suffocating and she became weaker and weaker. She was losing the battle. She was going to die at the hands of this awful man and she thought of her children, fatherless and soon to be motherless. There was barely time for a sob to escape before the world around her turned gray. Then black.

Skeeter wasn't aware that a neighbor was outside Gina's door, which was wide open, and saw him attack her, promptly called the cops and filmed the assault on his phone. The neighbor stood riveted to the spot, afraid to go in and help his neighbor, and fidgeted anxiously until he could hear the sirens approaching. All the while he prayed in Spanish for God to spare Gina, to save her from this maniac.

Skeeter heard the sirens, too, and he let go of Gina's throat abruptly. He jumped up, saw he'd left the door wide open, and saw the neighbor standing there still filming him as he came rushing out the door. He pushed the man aside and ran for his car and sped off.

The neighbor quickly ran into Gina's house to check on her. She was still alive but her breathing was shallow and her face was a bloody pulp. Two cops came charging into the house.

"Hands up!" they yelled.

The neighbor complied and told them he was the one who called them and that he had a picture of the man who beat Gina up. One cop went over to Gina and immediately called for an ambulance.

"Sit down, sir," said the other one." What's your name and relationship to Ms. Martinez?"

"I'm Jose Diego, her neighbor. We watch out for each other here. I always watch for Gina when she comes home because she's single and lives alone."

"Tell me what happened here tonight." So Diego told him and showed him the pictures he took. One clearly showed Joe's face as he was running out the door. Moments later the ambulance arrived and took Gina off to the hospital. The two police officers questioned Diego further about the assailant, but Diego had never seen the man before and had no idea who he was. He explained where Gina worked and suggested her boss might know if Gina was having trouble with any of the clients there. The officers thanked the man and departed.

Unaware of all that was happening to Gina, Maddie and Rick continued to munch their pizza, finish their Scrabble game (Rick won), and watch a movie. Maddie was sleeping more peacefully at night now, no more bad dreams, and woke up bright and chipper in the morning.

Driving into work, they were surprised to find policemen surrounding Marcia's desk, waiting to talk to Janie.

"What's going on?" they asked her.

"I don't know, but they were here before anybody else arrived," she whispered wide-eyed. "They asked to see Janie, but she'd called to say she'd be in late because of an early dental appointment, so they're waiting for her. I hope Janie gets here soon." Everyone already present and those arriving hovered around them, listening intently. Guesses and conjectures floated in the air but no one dared approach the police to question them.

Finally Janie arrived and Marcia pointed out the police officers waiting to see her. Janie went over and greeted them graciously, introduced herself, then asked them to follow her to her office. Her door remained closed for nearly fifteen minutes before Janie came out and motioned Maddie and Rick to join them. Inside, they learned about the vicious attack on Gina and that Skeeter nearly strangled her to death. Maddie's hands flew to her mouth and the blood drained from her face. It was all her fault! If Gina hadn't been protecting her. . .

She flopped down on the chair and cried. Rick filled everyone in on how Gina had stood up to Skeeter on Monday and Tuesday, stopping him from getting to Maddie. The police took down all the details.

"Ma'am, I'm Officer Bernie Rourke. I'm going to assign an officer to you to transport you around during the day until we catch up with this Skeeter. He's now facing assault charges on the two of you and attempted murder on Ms. Martinez. I understand Mr. Shelby here has been helpful at protecting you overnight at his place, which is fine—unless Skeeter figures out where that is and starts coming around. You look like you're in good physical shape, sir, and that you've already tangled with the guy, but I'm going to post a guard by your apartment building from 6:00 pm to 8:00 am as an added precaution."

"Would it be helpful for Maddie to take a few days off?" asked Janie.

"Actually, no, Ms. Cosgrove. I want to catch the guy trying to do something."

"You're going to use Maddie as bait?" she asked incredulously.

"Bait with protection around her day and night," he clarified. "We have to catch the guy doing something against the law in order to arrest him."

"Isn't the attack on Gina sufficient?"

Officer Rourke took a breath. "Absolutely. But the person he really wants is Ms. Roper, and unless he shows himself trying to get at her, we can't nab him. He was getting Ms. Martinez out of his way so he could get at Ms. Roper easier. So, yes, I need her to be visible, going about her daily routine to draw him out."

Janie looked at Maddie to see what she thought. Maddie looked at Rick. He shrugged, then nodded. "That sounds like a workable plan to me," said Rick. "I understand the logic of it. You have to be visible, Maddie. But you'll have someone with you at all times. Go with their plan."

Maddie sighed. "Okay," she agreed reluctantly, hating that she was at the center of so much attention. In spite of the proposed protection, she still remained fearful inside.

Officer Shirley Perkins arrived ten minutes later. She and Maddie shook hands and Maddie took note that the officer was toned and buffed. Definitely not a wimpy cop! They went into Maddie's office and Maddie discussed her schedule for the day with Perkins.

"Will you be coming inside the foster homes with me, Officer Perkins?" Maddie asked.

"Depends if you want me to or not. And, by the way, call me Shirley, or Shirl, or Perky, like everyone else while we're working together, and if it's okay with you I'll call you Maddie."

Maddie smiled and agreed. "My concern about you coming in with me is that it'll take the attention off the children, that you'll be the center of attention, or me, once they find out why you're there."

"Your call. I'm comfortable with it either way."

"Great. I think I'd rather you didn't because we're new to each other." Perkins nodded agreeably. "Well, let's head out then. I'd like to get two visits in yet this morning and go visit Gina in the hospital."

They went first to see Dawn Durant, who'd been placed in her foster home yesterday. Maddie didn't know these foster parents so she was glad Shirley wouldn't be going in with her. Shirley pulled up in front of the house and waited for instructions.

Maddie explained she'd go in alone and would take about twenty minutes or so.

"I don't see Joe's Silverado anywhere around so maybe the morning will stay nice and calm like this. After lunch, we'll run up to the hospital to see Gina."

"That's fine with me. See you in twenty minutes or so."

"If the foster mother is a talker, it may take longer, but no more than thirty or forty. See you shortly."

Maddie looked around before getting out of the car. The coast was clear but she hurried up to the door anyway and rang the bell. One of the foster children opened it and let her in. Maddie met Dory Fletcher, the foster mother and visited with her for a while, then sat down with Dawn in her bedroom and checked on how she was doing.

"It's not what I expected," Dawn confessed. "I expected Dory to be like my mom and she's not. Oh, she's nice and all, just not warm and fuzzy."

"But your adjusting and doing alright?"

"Yeah. I made friends with Delaney, one of the other foster girls here, the cutest black girl I've ever met. She's got dimples and kinky-curly hair and laughs a lot." Dawn chatted on about Delaney and school and life in the foster home. She seemed to be adjusting to it just fine. After lots of hugs and reassurances, Maddie yelled goodbye to Ms. Fletcher, checked out the window by the door to make sure Shirley was still there and Joe wasn't.

She hurried to the car and climbed in. She smiled at Shirley, then backed up to the car door and screamed. The officer was bleeding profusely from the head! Blood was everywhere! She was also unconscious. Suddenly an arm reached over the front seat and grabbed Maddie around the neck. She yelped and squirmed and fought, fighting to get her door opened at the same time so she could run once she slipped out from under Joe's hold on her. She was just about free when he grabbed a handful of her hair, yanking her back. Screaming, she pulled with all her might and left the hank of hair behind as she managed to get away from him and out of the car. Running and crying, she rushed back to the foster home and banged on the door. But Joe came up behind her and grabbed her around the waist and carried her over to his car and threw her in the back seat. She hit her head on the window so hard it stunned her just long enough that he had time to get in the car and click the locks down. The foster mother opened the door in time to see Joe drive off and quickly called the police. In the car, Maddie cried and banged on Joe's shoulders and head and begged him to let her go.

"Not now, not ever!" he roared and sped crazily through the streets until he was out of town and driving up a deserted road into the mountains. When he came to a lane cutting off to the right he turned onto it, pulled the car into the trees, and turned it off. Maddie pushed herself away from Joe as far back in the seat as she could get. As soon as he unlocked the doors to get out, she planned to run like the devil as far away from him as possible. But he didn't unlock the doors. Instead he turned around in his seat and reached for Maddie. She scooted further from him, trying to will herself into a tiny ball that he couldn't reach but he grabbed her coat, pulling her inexorably closer and closer. She fought him with all the strength she could muster, pulling back, scratching him, digging her fingernails into his skin, anything she could think of. Suddenly he pulled her coat so hard toward him that the buttons popped off. Urgently, she tried to get away but he latched onto her hand with an iron grip and held on, pulling her closer and closer to him.

"No!" she cried. "Joe, stop this! Please, you're hurting me!"

"And I haven't even started yet, bitch!"

The next thing Maddie knew, Joe had crawled over the front seat into the back with her, laying heavily on top of her, forcing his tongue into her mouth until she nearly choked. She bit it as hard as she could and he yanked it out and slapped her. He then backhanded her over and over, bloodying her nose and mouth.

Still she tried to reason with him, to talk him out of what he was doing, but he was too busy trying to get her clothes off of her to pay attention. She cried and she yelled for help but only got slapped some more for her efforts. Finally, he had all of her clothes off. Yanking his pants down he went into her as hard as he could. Maddie screamed until Joe cut it short by covering her mouth and nose with his free hand. Maddie couldn't breathe. He held his hand there until she passed out.

She woke up off and on during the unrelenting assault on her body until she didn't care if she lived or died. There was pain everywhere. And blood. She prayed for the horror to end, for Joe to come to his senses and stop. At last, her world went dark for a very long time.

When she woke up some time later, it was early evening and she was laying out on the ground, buck naked and freezing cold. Joe was gone. The pain was so bad; consciousness came and went; and she lay there until the cold took over her mind. But then, a tiny little warning bell went off in her brain. A small but persistent voice told her to get up, move, that if she didn't she would surely die. Stirring ever so carefully, to avoid the sharpness of the pain, she slowly stretched out on the ground and looked around. Where was she anyway? How would she get back home? She didn't have her phone anymore to call for help, filling her with more fear and despair.

With a mighty effort, screaming and crying from the pain, she made herself get up. Shaking but holding herself stiffly to avoid stabs of pain, she took a tiny step forward. Then another one. Slowly, step by step, she began walking. After several minutes she stopped and turned around in a circle so she could see where the lights of the city were and then aimed herself in that direction. Inch by inch, she plodded forward until she got up to the road they had turned off of. It was just a mountain road and she looked both ways for signs of traffic. Nothing was in sight in either direction. She prayed for a car to come along and help her.

So cold. So very cold! She walked with her arms crossed over her chest trying to hold some heat in but everything about her felt like ice. She'd walked for perhaps ten minutes when she stumbled. Crying from the pain, she made herself get up and plod on. Then she stumbled again and had to force herself to get up. It hurt so bad! The third time she fell, she sat and broke into tears. She couldn't find the energy to get back up. However, after sitting there for several minutes and shivering uncontrollably, she finally managed to do it through sheer will power.

More time passed and darkness was descending in earnest. Suddenly, she thought she saw a car coming down the road toward her. She eagerly watched it come closer, but then it turned off onto another road and disappeared. She wilted and dropped down to the ground and bawled. She laid down and curled into a fetal position, giving up. She was so cold, so tired. Closing her eyes, she prayed that God would take her quickly and take care of her parents and Rick.

It was three days later when she next opened her eyes and found herself in a warm, comfortable bed in a hospital room filled with many, many vases of flowers. An IV dripped in her arm and a cannula pushed oxygen into her nose. As she surveyed her surroundings, her eyes finally lighted on Rick snoozing in a recliner nearby. She tried to smile—she was alive, she'd survived!—but her face hurt too much. Nor did she have any memory of how she got from that barren, deserted road to the hospital, but she was enormously grateful and sent a prayer of thanks up to God for saving her.

She closed her eyes again and rested, tears of happiness cursing down her cheeks. When she woke the next time, her parents were sitting in her room quietly talking between themselves.

"Hi, Mom. Hi, Dad," she said, though her voice came out as a croak.

They rushed to her side, taking her hands and caressing her cheeks. Lucy was crying and trying to smile at the same time.

"Oh, my poor darling!"

"I'm okay, Mom. I'm alive. I don't know who found me and brought me here, but I am eternally grateful to that person."

"Someone spotted what they thought was the body lying on the side of the road and called the police. Rick was there when the call came in and raced the cops out to get you."

"Oh, Mom, what about Shirley, Officer Perkins? I found her bleeding from her head in her car when I came out of the foster home."

"She's going to live. Joe hit her with something really hard, probably a rock, cut her head open and gave her a concussion. She's okay, but she's hopping mad."

"I bet! And what about Gina?"

"Gina's going to be alright, too. Oh, honey! Joe did terrible things to you! You had to have surgery to undo some of the damage done to you. I will never forgive him for stripping you and leaving you to die from loss of blood and exposure!"

Maddie turned away. "I don't want to talk about it right now, Mom."

Her father came around to the other side of the bed. "Mads, the police have alerted every jurisdiction in Colorado to be on the lookout for Joe. He won't get away with what he did."

Maddie nodded but closed her eyes, not wanting to think or talk about what had happened. She sensed her parents leaving later and someone else coming in. She prayed it was Rick because she didn't feel up to dealing with anyone else at the moment. He came over to her and softly placed a kiss on her cheek. Her eyes flew open.

"Hi," he whispered, a concerned smile on his face. "I didn't mean to disturb you." He sat down on the side of her bed and held her hand. "I've got the night shift," he explained. "You can go back to sleep."

"I was just pretending to sleep. I didn't feel like dealing with my parents."

"They mean well, Maddie. They love you. They're very worried about you."

"I know, but sometimes it feels like smother love."

"That's because you're so precious to them." He gently rubbed her hand and studied the bruises and cuts on her face.

"I look ugly, don't I? He really beat me up."

"The bruises will go away. What I'm concerned about is everything else he did to you. The police have been waiting patiently to talk to you and get your statement." He hesitated a moment then asked quietly, "Do you want to talk about it with me first?"

"No! It was horrible, Rick! I don't know if I even remember everything he did to me. A lot of it is fuzzy, especially at the end. I don't remember him putting me outside the car and driving off." Rick squeezed her hand.

"You going to have to tell the police sooner or later, Maddie. Why don't you start putting it into words now?" he coaxed.

Maddie teared up but began telling him about finding Officer Perkins bleeding badly from the head, then Joe reaching over the front seat and grabbing her, and on through the rest of the story. Rick sat in silence at the end of her recitation, an intense anger inside him at the abuse she had taken from Joe.

"I thought I was going to die out there in the cold," she said. "But someone saw me and called the police?"

"Yeah. I happened to be there when the call came in and raced the police to get to you first, but they beat me. We all wrapped our coats around you until the ambulance got there and you were rushed to the hospital. I've heard the preliminary report from the doctor when he told your parents all the things that Joe had done to you." Rick thought of the internal damage and had to stop talking and look away from Maddie. "I should have been there for you."

"Rick, look at me." Reluctantly he turned and faced her. "You got to me before I died and you're here with me now. That's what matters. We had a good protection plan worked out, but I guess we underestimated Joe. Oh! I just remembered! Joe wasn't driving his Silverado when he grabbed me. It was a different car, a regular sedan. I think it was an Accord, or a car like that."

"Wonderful! That's important information! Be sure to tell the cops when they get here." Rick grinned at her then. "That's my Maddie," he said and gently caressed her swollen cheek.

Maddie scooted herself up in bed then closed her eyes and groaned. Everything hurt. "I wish the police would come now. I'd like to tell them what they need to know and get it over with."

"Let me tell the guard outside the door."

When he returned, he told her an officer would be over shortly to get her statement. "And tell him everything, Maddie," he urged. "Try to remember as much as you can. And about the car."

Two officers arrived ten minutes later.

"Remember me, Ms. Roper? I'm Officer Rourke and this is my partner, Officer Claymore. She's taking Officer Perkins place for a while."

"Yes, I remember you," Maddie answered him. "Nice to meet you Officer Claymore."

During the next twenty minutes, the two officers gently led Maddie through the whole incident, taking copious notes. They got the medical report from the doctor regarding the extensive internal injuries she sustained, told her they'd be back to ask more questions at another time, then shook her hand and departed.

Maddie shifted carefully back down in her bed.

"Want anything to eat or drink?" asked Rick.

"Something to drink. Cold and creamy."

"I'll see what I can do," he said and left the room. Two minutes later, he returned with a chocolate Ensure and a straw and watched her sip it greedily.

"Ah, that was refreshing. Rick?"

"Yes?"

"I'm alive! I don't care how badly Joe hurt me, I'm alive to tell about it. God is good! He heard my prayer and He rescued me. He sent a Good Samaritan who called the police, then He sent you and the police to bring me home. I thank God for His mercy, and I thank you, Rick, for caring about me. You hardly know me, but you've been my friend and supporter since the day I met you."

Rick just gave her a crooked smile and an aw-shucks look. "Guess I'm just a rescuer at heart like you," he said quietly.

They sat quietly after that and eventually Maddie drifted off to sleep. Rick went over to the recliner and got as comfortable as he could to keep vigil through the night. He found himself mulling over her last words. He had a hard time understanding how she could be so thankful for being alive after having her insides torn up and her chances of ever having children ruined. She almost froze to death out there, yet she praised God and everyone who had made it possible for her to be rescued. What faith! He thought of his own faith and, compared to Maddie's, found it sorely lacking. Instead, he was full of rage at Joe, could even picture himself beating the man to a pulp—or worse.

Sighing, he glanced over at Maddie resting peacefully. She was such a beautiful person, he thought, with a beauty inside that radiated out. She was the kindest, most loving and forgiving person he'd ever met. With those thoughts swirling in his mind, he dozed off.

CHAPTER 11

More Retaliation

MADDIE MISSED OUT ON Thanksgiving dinner since she'd still been heavily sedated and unconscious. Her parents and Rick decided to make up for it on Sunday by bringing her a plate of turkey, dressing, green bean casserole, mashed potatoes, candied yams, and a slice of pumpkin pie. Maddie had a hard time opening her mouth wide enough to get the food in and it was painful to chew but she did the best she could and tried a bite of everything, then thanked her parents and Rick profusely. Lucy fussed over how little she'd eaten but Maddie turned to her father.

"How did church go this morning?" she asked him.

"Fine," he replied. "It's the first Sunday in Advent, you know. The tree's up, but not fully decorated yet. That'll happen Wednesday after choir practice. The children are practicing for their pageant on the sixteenth. The choir's gearing up for their cantata on the twenty-third, with hand-bells. But, of course, everybody and their brother keep asking me about you. Some knew you'd been injured, but not how, some think you're in the hospital for an operation, most just know you're in the hospital.

I didn't reveal anything, Mads, but I did assure them you going to be okay."

Maddie took an extended sick leave from work and recuperated at her parents' home when she was discharged the following Wednesday. Rick stopped by every evening and had dinner with them and filled Maddie in on her cases, which were being covered by two of her teammates, Ida Cooper and Rosie Marshall. He also reported on the health and recuperation of Gina Martinez and Officer Shirley Perkins. Maddie was eternally grateful Joe hadn't killed them. She wanted to know if the police had caught up with him yet, and Rick told her no, but that Skeeter'd been sighted in various different places in the area.

"You know," she said as she and Rick were sitting in the living room one evening, "I don't hate Joe for what he did to me. I don't understand his terrible rage at me, but. . ."

Rick turned to her sharply. How could she not hate the monster for what he did to her?

"I agree with you, Rick," she went on. "I think he's mentally ill. He has a sickness and the things he does are not willful acts. I think he's hurting so bad inside he can only express himself by hurting others. I'm afraid he's also going to hurt himself one day if he continues this way."

"Let the police deal with him. It's not your concern anymore."

"But I still care about him, Rick. I loved him at one point."

Rick took her hands. "The man is out of control. He's dangerous. This is a matter for the police, not a social worker, even if she is the lovingist person on the face of this earth. You can't save him, Maddie, if he doesn't want to be saved."

Maddie didn't want that to be true, but she knew it was.

"Please. Don't seek him out," Rick continued. "You can't reason with the guy. You can't trust him not to hurt you again."

She nodded reluctantly. "Poor Joe," she said and let Rick put his arm around her and draw her close to him. He wanted to shout, "Well poor Joe nearly killed you!" but held his peace.

With great difficulty. Instead, he concentrated on helping her relax before he had to leave to go home.

When her sick leave was up, Maddie got herself dressed and ready to go back to work. It was now the middle of December and snow blanketed the city and capped the mountains. Officer Ruth Claymore would be picking her up and she prayed nothing would happen to her like what happened to Shirley Perkins.

She still hurt badly but she felt she needed to get back to her cases and feel functional again. The activity would get some of the kinks out, she hoped. Claymore rang the doorbell of the parsonage and escorted Maddie to the car.

"I'm Ruth," she told Maddie. "We're sticking together like glue, okay? I'm not leaving your side. Sorry if it cramps your style, but you'll just have to deal with it."

"Okay," answered Maddie. She studied Ruth surreptitiously as she pulled away from the curb. Dark hair and eyes, a hard look on her face, strong-looking arms. No warm fuzzies or smiles like Shirley. Ah well. Maybe it was for the best.

When she walked through the door at CPS, she was greeted more warmly than she expected. At Marcia's desk, she got mobbed by her teammates, all asking her questions at the same time. Laughing and reassuring them she was fine and glad to be back to work, she made her way to her office with Ruth Claymore right on her heels.

Inside, she sat at her desk. She noticed immediately that someone had dusted the office (she'd been out for nearly four weeks) and placed a vase with roses in it to welcome her back. She was overwhelmed by the gestures of kindness. Ida Cooper and Rosie Marshall knocked on her open door and entered, greeting her with hugs and questions about her health.

"I'm fine," she assured them. "Tell me about my cases that you covered." So they filled her in and handed her the case files with all their typed notes.

Maddie grinned at them. "You two are amazing! Thank you so much for helping me out."

Ida and Rosie exchanged looks, then glanced at Ruth standing off to one side, then turned back to Maddie.

Ida said, "We heard your ex-husband beat the shit out of you and left you for dead. Is that true?"

Maddie's grin faltered and she sat back in her chair. Ruth stepped forward and in a less than friendly voice asked the two workers to leave. They did, but threw the officer a dirty look. Ruth closed the door firmly behind them.

"You don't need to answer those kinds of questions, Ms. Roper," she said.

"I know, I wasn't going to. Please call me Maddie like everyone else does."

"Okay, Maddie. What's next?

"I need to talk to my supervisor, Janie Cosgrove. She's just down the hall." Ruth opened the door and they went down to Janie's office.

"Maddie! Come in!" exclaimed Janie and got up to hug her.

"Janie, this is Officer Ruth Claymore who's going to transport me around everywhere. How's Gina doing, do you know?"

"I know she's home and her sister, Jasmine, is there staying with her. Jasmine is bigger and stronger than Gina and I don't think anyone will get to Gina with her there." Janie chuckled. "And I hear that Officer Perkins is home also and doing fine."

"Thank goodness!"

"Now tell me how you're doing, Maddie."

"I'm getting better. Not in as much pain. I'm alright, Janie." She smiled at her and Janie took her hands and gave them a squeeze. Feelings of sorrow, worry, and concern shown on Janie's face, who then turned to Ruth.

"Please take good care of her," she said.

"I'll do my best, Ms. Cosgrove. She won't get hurt on my watch, I promise."

Later, Ruth took Maddie to see some of her foster kids, but Maddie tired easily that first day and got permission to go home early. Ruth dropped her off at her parents' home and promised to be back the next morning at 7:45 sharp.

Maddie wondered how Rick was doing. She hadn't seen him all day and waited eagerly for him to come over for dinner and visit. But dinnertime came and went and no Rick showed up. She tried dialing him several times but it always went to voicemail. Getting alarmed, she called Officer Rourke and asked him to check on Rick and see if he was okay.

Fifteen minutes later, the phone rang and Officer Rourke reported Rick was not at home and nobody had seen him since last night when he got home from her place. Fear sprung up inside of Maddie. Oh God, she thought. Not Rick, too! Joe couldn't—he wouldn't have! But deep in her heart, she knew he could and would. All of a sudden she felt cold all over with fear for Rick.

"We're going to find him, Maddie," promised Rourke. "I'll call you as soon as I know something."

The Ropers sat in the living room with Maddie while she waited for Rourke to call back. The TV was on, the sound muted. They stared at the talking faces and at each other. Maddie kept her phone handy in readiness. Two hours went by before it rang.

"We found his car," said Rourke, "but there's no sign of Rick." More quietly he added, "We also found blood on the driver's seat and side window. Stay right where you are, Maddie. Do not leave your parents' home. I'm sending two patrol cars over there for your protection." Maddie started moaning and rocking, her fear for Rick overwhelming her.

Maddie didn't sleep a wink that night, certain beyond measure that Rick was badly hurt somewhere and no one knew where. She berated herself for getting him involved in her affairs. She prayed fervently that God would save him like He saved her.

It was the next morning before they heard from Rourke again. "We found him, Maddie. He's on his way to the hospital as we speak. He's in bad shape but he's young and strong. He'll pull through." Maddie plied him for details but he cut her off, saying he'd stop by later to talk to her. She wanted to rush to the hospital to be with Rick, but Rourke told her to wait until at least tomorrow. Rick would be prepped for surgery as soon as he got there and he'd be heavily sedated for a day or two afterwards, to give his body time to start to heal. It would probably be Friday before he'd wake up.

Beside herself with worry, she knew she wouldn't be able to concentrate on her cases that day so she called Janie to tell her what had happened to Rick and that she'd be taking the day off. All day she moped around, alternately crying for Rick or manically cleaning house for her mother. Rourke called her that night to tell her the surgery was successful and that Rick was now in a medically-induced coma for the time being. Her parents tried in vain to console her, but she wasn't interested in consolation. Instead, she asked her father to offer prayers up for Rick, Gina and Shirley and he put his whole heart and soul into it for Maddie's sake. Maddie cried herself to sleep that night, blaming herself for all the trouble she was bringing to the people she cared about. Lucy insisted she take a sleeping pill so she could sleep and stayed with her until she finally drifted off.

The next morning, she had Ruth rush her to the hospital to check on Rick.

In the ICU, she was directed to his cubicle where a policeman sat. He knew Ruth and let them in. Maddie froze when she saw Rick. He was unrecognizable. His face was a mass of bruises, welts, and long stitched-up cuts. An arm and a leg were in casts and he was hooked up to an IV and an oxygen machine. Maddie became lightheaded at the sight of him and Ruth caught her as she started to faint and sat her in a nearby chair.

Ruth pressed the nurse's buzzer on Rick's bed and a nurse came in. Ruth asked for a glass of water for Maddie and for the doctor to come in and talk to them.

Shortly, Dr. Robert Usutu arrived. He acknowledged Ruth and then turned his attention to Maddie. "I remember you from when you were a patient here," he said, "and I recognized Rick from his visits to your room. I'll get right to the point, Ms. Roper. Your boyfriend took one hell of a beating. If he wasn't in as good a shape as he is, he would have died from it. His injuries are too numerous to name. I worked on him for hours in surgery putting him back together. He's going to make it, although it will take months of therapy to get all the parts of his body working well again. As for mentally, I don't know. There's been some brain damage. The guy who did this to him should be shot, hung and quartered! Literally! It's the worst beating I've ever seen and I've seen plenty from working in emergency rooms. The good news is that he has a support system in you and your family, as well as his family who are on their way here as we speak. He'll need all the support you can give him to get through the grueling physical therapy to come. For now, he needs to rest and to heal." He smiled at Maddie, trying to reassure her, but he saw the fear and the anguish in her eyes. "I'll keep you posted," he said patting her on the shoulder, and left.

Ruth, sensing Maddie wanted to be alone with Rick for a few minutes, went out and visited with the guard at Rick's door.

Maddie scooted her chair closer to Rick's bed and wanted to hold his hand but was afraid to touch him for fear of hurting him. Not to mention there was hardly any skin visible, since everything was wrapped up in bandages or in a cast. She cried silent tears for him, blaming herself for the beating he took from Joe. Why couldn't the police have caught Joe before he hurt Rick? Her thoughts immediately jumped to her parents. They weren't as young and vigorous as Gina, Shirley, Rick, or herself. And Joe, in his warped mind, could want to "punish" them too for keeping Maddie away from him.

Pushing back from the bed and standing close to the door, she dialed her parents' home. Her father answered. He asked about

Rick right away and she told him what the doctor had told her. Then she asked if the two patrolmen were still outside of the parsonage. Roper went to the window and peeked and assured Maddie they were.

"Please be careful," she whispered as she said goodbye.

She called Janie next to fill her in on Rick's condition, then she went back to sit by Rick's bedside to pray for his healing. His parents, John and Martha, and two brothers, Peter and George, arrived later that day and Maddie and the Shelby family rotated visiting times so someone would always be there when he finally awoke.

Eventually, the doctor began weaning Rick off the heavy drugs he was on so he could begin to wake up. It was Christmas Eve and Maddie was sitting by his bed at the time holding his only undamaged finger when he opened his eyes. He looked around, trying to make sense of where he was and what had happened. When his eyes lighted on Maddie, there was no recognition of who she was at first. She gave his hand a couple of squeezes and he blinked, while continuing to stare at her. Finally, his frown disappeared as recognition dawned and he tried to smile at her.

"Welcome back, Rick!" she exclaimed. "It's Christmas and your waking up is the best present I ever received! Your parents are here, too, but down getting something to eat at the moment. I'm so glad you made it back!"

"I thought for sure I'd wake up in heaven, not still here on earth," he mumbled, his words slightly slurred.

"This is heaven!" she asserted. "You're alive! The other heaven can wait. I want you here on earth for a while."

"Good," he mumbled, a slight smile on his face as his eyelids drooped and he slid back into sleep. As soon as the Shelbys returned to the room, Maddie happily filled them in. They hugged each other and Maddie slipped away so the Shelbys could have their visit. Ruth took her home and bid her a Merry Christmas and a good night.

Each evening Maddie visited Rick, he grew stronger and stayed awake longer. Maddie tried to get him to tell her what Joe had done to him but he shook his head. "I told the cops. I don't feel like repeating it."

"You coaxed me to talk about my ordeal. I'm coaxing you now to tell me about yours."

"Maybe later," he replied. "I will say the man is definitely totally crazy and has the strength of a gorilla. He's vicious and cruel and the only thought in his mind is to do as much damage as possible without actually killing the person, though I thought sure I was going to die more than once. But," he went on, changing the subject, "tell me, how things are going with you, Maddie?"

She frowned at him. "Rick Shelby, you're impossible!" Then she lightened-up. "Things are going as well as can be expected," she told him, "with a cop shadowing me everywhere I go, Janie restricting my caseload to keep me in the building more, and cops all around my parents' place and everywhere they go. We're doing fine under the circumstances. It's you I'm worried about, Rick. I want you to heal and get better and be your old self again."

"Yeah, me, too. The doc says I'll be in therapy for months to get back in shape, but that's alright. At least I'm alive to do it. Maddie, I'm sorry I underestimated Joe. I'm sorry that you and Gina and Shirley got hurt so bad, but I'm grateful you all pulled through."

"You, too, Rick," she said. "Don't forget yourself." He let out a sigh and turned away from her. She could tell he was in a great deal of pain.

"Look," he said, turning back to her. "I've been talking with my parents and I think I'll go home with them when I get released from the hospital here, for the therapy. I won't be able work for a long time and support myself. And-and I'm not sure I'll be back."

Maddie's breath caught. "Rick! No! Stay here. My parents and I will take care of you. Don't go."

He reached for her hand. "I failed you, Maddie. I thought I could handle Joe and I couldn't."

"We all failed, then, Rick! Me, Gina, Shirley, the police. None of us managed to do any better. I don't want you to leave, Rick. I've come to. . .to care about you a lot. I like having you around."

"I'm a mess right now, Maddie. I'm no use to you."

"But I need you."

"Need me?" he repeated, searching her eyes. She nodded, tears glistening. He reached his almost good arm up and gently brushed her tears away. "Don't cry, Maddie. I'll stay if you want me to."

"Yes," she whispered, "I want you to."

She leaned forward then and kissed him under his left eye, the only spot on his face without a bandage or stitches. He accepted her kiss and wished he could wrap an arm around her and hold her tight.

"I love you, Maddie," he whispered. "I just thought I'd let you down so badly you'd want me to leave."

"Not a chance!" she told him emphatically. "You're the best thing that's ever happened to me! I love you, too."

After church on Sunday, while Maddie and the Shelbys were all in the room with Rick, Officer Rourke entered, a big grin on his ruddy face.

"Happy New Year! I have great news!" he announced. "We caught Skeeter! He was hanging around your parents' place, Maddie, looking for a way in. He thought the cops had gone because he didn't see them guarding the house, but they were there. I had them use different cars and park in different places on the street. They rushed him as soon as he tried to break a window to get inside the parsonage, and believe me, it took all four of my strongest guys to subdue him and get him into a squad car! He's cooling his heels in a holding cell right now and we're in the process of informing Gina Martinez and Officer Shirley Perkins that he's been caught. You can now breathe a huge sigh of relief, everyone, because this maniac is off the streets." Rourke was grinning from ear to ear. Maddie and Rick's family got all excited that the nightmare was over and she squeezed Rick's hand and held on tight.

Rick closed his eyes, more relieved than he would ever let on. Immobilized like he was, he knew he was no good to Maddie, but now he could let the tension ease out of his body and begin to concentrate on his own healing.

The Ropers called to tell their version of the story and to express their immense relief also that they could get back to living normally again. Maddie had her phone on speaker and she could hear her mother sobbing in the background.

"Give Mom a hug for me, Dad, will you? I'll be home a little later. It's going to be a very happy New Year after all!"

Everyone thanked Rourke for his great work in catching Joe. He saluted them, wished them all a happy holiday season, and left.

The Shelbys offered to take Maddie home later that night and she accepted. She thanked Ruth profusely for all she'd done to keep her safe and sent her on her way. She took a moment to kiss Rick goodnight before she left.

Rick lay in bed a long time afterwards contemplating everything as his parents dozed. He especially thought about Maddie. A smile creeped up his face. He'd found the woman of his dreams! He thought about what she'd said when she got home from the hospital after Joe had so savagely hurt her, that she was grateful to God, that she felt blessed that she had been rescued and was alive. Did he feel blessed, too? Of course he was glad he'd survived, no question about that, and he was grateful that Maddie wanted him to stay and accepted his love for her. But, blessed? With months of therapy stretching out ahead of him and the constant headache he quietly endured? Hospitalized was not where he expected to be for the holidays. Yet, he was alive and Joe was no longer a threat. He guessed he could call them blessings. And Maddie. Yeah, Maddie was decidedly a blessing. Feeling a lightness inside him he'd seldom ever felt, he raised his eyes heavenward and realized just how blessed he truly was. His smile deepened. His last thoughts were of God's kindness and Maddie's love as he drifted off to sleep.

CHAPTER 12

Prepping

WHILE JOE WAS ARGUING with his court-appointed attorney on Monday and insisting that he did nothing wrong, that he only wanted to scare Maddie into returning to him, Maddie's life was returning to normal. She carried her full caseload again, went out on her home visits, appeared in court to advocate for her children, and visited Rick at the hospital. She spent that night, New Year's Eve, in the hospital with him, snuggling the best she could on the narrow bed. He was careful not to bump her with his casts and barely slept a wink all night to make sure he didn't.

The next day he started out the New Year by moving out of the ICU to a private room. Two weeks later he was transferred to the Ropers' home until the casts could come off and he could manage on his own in his own apartment. Two weeks after that, the casts were removed and physical therapy began in earnest at an outpatient rehab center. Roper or Lucy drove him there until he could get permission to drive his own car again.

Maddie visited him at the rehab center, watching him struggle to get his broken leg and arm strong again and dexterity back in his badly damaged hands. She saw the sweat pour off him as he pushed himself, determined to become the man he used to be. At first he was self-conscious with Maddie watching him, then he found he looked forward to her visits because she always encouraged him, praised him for reaching each goal he and his trainer set, and rewarded him with smiles and kisses. What more could he ask for?

One day during a short break, Rick asked Maddie about work, if he'd have a job there again when he was able to return. Maddie promised to find out and the very next morning she approached Janie with his question.

"Of course he will," Janie assured her. "There are always openings here, so even if he doesn't get the same position he had, there will definitely be a place for him."

Maddie happily relayed the message to Rick later that day and he smiled with relief. He went back to his workout and Maddie watched and gave him a thumbs-up sign whenever he looked over at her.

He had lost quite a bit of weight she noticed and worried about that. Wasn't he eating enough? Or was he just working out so hard he burned too many calories? His face glistened with sweat. She watched his therapist, a big, muscular, oriental man, who never let Rick slow down or take a rest when she thought he should have. The guy just kept pushing Rick to do more and to do it better and faster.

Rick showered and got dressed when he was done and Maddie took him home to the parsonage. He looked tired and flopped back on the seat, eyes closed.

"He really pushes you," commented Maddie.

"Yeah," he agreed, "but that's the only way I'll get my strength back. I feel as weak as a kitten sometimes." He sat up and commented. "I like having you around, Maddie. You inspire me to keep going. If I'd gone home with my parents, my mother would be scolding Kim right now for making me work so hard. I get encouragement, hugs and kisses from you. Much better!" He grinned at her and she returned it.

"I love you, Maddie. I promise not to hurt you in any way. I have a feeling you put up with a lot more from Joe than you've let on. Compared to what I went through, I know he had to have hurt you in many, many ways. You're just such a loving, forgiving kind of person you've minimized it."

Maddie looked away from Rick, then back. "It's doesn't matter anymore, Rick. Joe won't be able to get to me again, and as far as what he did to me in the past, that's up to God to deal with. I've turned it all over to God."

"You're amazing, Maddie. You're the most loving, forgiving person I've ever met."

"I'm just so glad we both survived. God was watching out for us." She pulled into the parking lot between the church and the parsonage and they headed inside.

The following Monday, a young teenaged couple showed up at CPS and headed for Marcia's desk. They asked for Maddie and Marcia called her. Maddie went out to greet them and saw a pretty blond-headed girl and a handsome young black man holding hands and looking anxious.

"Can I help you?" she asked them. They looked at each other, then back at Maddie. The girl spoke.

"You probably don't remember me, Maddie, but I met you one time nearly two years ago when you brought your youth group over to my church to meet with my youth group. I was so impressed with you. You genuinely accepted the blacks in both our groups without batting an eyelash."

"I think I remember," commented Maddie thoughtfully. "Listen, let's go down to my office where we won't be disturbing the other workers. We can talk there." On the way, Maddie had a glimmer of an idea of why they were here and why a certain little brown baby was left at her church for her to find nearly three months ago.

She pulled an extra chair in and invited them to sit. "Why don't you begin by telling me your names, please," she suggested.

"I'm Veronica Harper, Roni for short, and this is my boyfriend, my fiancé, Neil Jefferson. We—we got pregnant and my mother made me leave the house because my baby would be a mixed-race baby. Neil's parents weren't too happy about it either, but they let me stay with them until I began to show. Then they put me up in a motel and Neil moved in with me when the baby became due. We delivered the baby ourselves. We read about how to do that on the Internet and it went okay, although it hurt a whole lot more than I expected. Anyway, we were afraid and didn't know what to do with the baby. We're both still in high school, our senior year. Then I remembered you and I knew you were a social worker, so I thought you'd take the baby and find a good home for it, I mean her. Only now," she went on, beginning to cry, "we don't want to give the baby up. Is it too late to get her back?"

"No, Roni, it's not too late," answered Maddie kindly. "An abandoned baby is kept for a substantial amount of time in case the mother changes her mind, like you have. We've named her Susie Q, by the way, and she's beautiful! She's in a delightful foster home with two loving foster parents. I'm sure you'll have to go through a battery of tests to convince the judge that you can support her and provide a decent place for her to live in. Are either of you working?"

"We both have part-time jobs," answered Neal. "And I think my parents will help us get a small apartment to live in if we get her back."

"A good support system is important. What about your parents, Roni?"

"There won't be much help coming from them," she answered bitterly. "They may be Christians, but they're as prejudiced as they come."

"Are you planning to finish high school? Or going on to college?"

"Yes to finishing high school," answered Roni, "then I'll keep my part-time job, if I get my baby back, while Neal goes on to the university, otherwise a fulltime job. He's got scholarships already lined up. Maybe later I'll take some classes too, once my daughter is in Kindergarten."

"Okay," said Maddie. "Wait here while I go talk to my supervisor. I'll be right back."

After filling Janie in, Janie asked her to escort the young couple to her office and she'd talk with them. Maddie knew they'd have a sympathetic ear in Janie, a mixed-race lady herself, and she silently wished the young couple well. On her way back to her office she noticed Marcia and a couple of the workers hanging about watching her, so she went over and explained that the couple were the parents of Baby Susie Q and were going to try to get her back.

Then she got back to reviewing her cases. The Durants were improving. Fred Durant had started coming back to church with Mimi and he was now included in the family visits. He'd begun to understand how harsh he'd been on Dawn by blaming her for what Ollie did to her, and finally admitted to having had a terrible day at the office and bringing his anger home with him. He had agreed to apologize to Dawn and they were becoming a family again.

The Bermans had their children back and things were going well there. The case could be closed soon. The Ordmans were working diligently on learning new ways to discipline Clarissa without beating her. Maddie did note on one parent-child visit between Amelia and Clarissa that Amelia was yanking pretty hard on Clarissa's hair as she braided it, to the point where Clarissa was crying silently. Maddie sent Clarissa out to the playroom for a few minutes when they were done while she spoke to Amelia.

"Are you aware of how much you were hurting your daughter while you did her hair, Amelia?"

"Yes. Life is hard for us blacks and she needs to get used to it." She gave Maddie a defiant look. "It was hard for me and George growing up, too, you know. Our parents used switches and branches on us, made us get them ourselves for the beatings. Clarissa can put up with a little pain, too, so she gets used to it."

Quietly, Maddie told her, "What you and George went through was just as abusive as the beating George gave Clarissa in Germany. But because you were abused doesn't give you the right to be abusive too. What Clarissa needs from you is kindness and love and support for the times when others mistreat her, or berate her, or call her nigger and other hurtful names. She needs a home where she can get sympathy and understanding from her parents, not more abuse." Taking a breath, Maddie added, "I don't ever want to see you deliberating hurting Clarissa again, Amelia."

Amelia glared at her but Maddie held her ground.

Maddie said, "The word discipline means teaching, you know, or correction. It does not mean hurting."

"What about 'spare the rod and spoil the child'?" retorted Amelia.

"The 'rod,'" explained Maddie, glad for her Christian background, "was used to draw sheep back from wandering away. It was meant to protect them and keep them safe. It was not used to hit them."

She and Amelia studied each other for a long moment. Finally Amelia looked away and sighed. "I've got so much to learn, don't I?" she said, resigned.

"We all do, Amelia. No one gave out guidebooks to parents and those that are out there seem to contradict each other. We just do the best we can."

"Thank you, Maddie. I'll try to do better."

She checked next on the Stuart children, Cory, Julie and Mikey, who were doing well in the foster home. David Stuart continued to have a drinking problem, however. At one point he called up his military social worker at Fort Carson while very drunk and made terroristic threats to her and Maddie. He was currently in jail awaiting trial. Mary Stuart continued to visit her children on a regular basis but remained hostile to Maddie and anyone else from CPS.

Checking on Candy Aberdeen, the fifteen-year old who claimed to have been sexually abused by a coven of witches, she called Elena Menendez, her foster mother, for a report. Elena was a friend of the family who went through foster care training to foster Candy. She took a no-nonsense approach to Candy and what she considered her histrionics. Elena reported a second episode where Candy claimed she was taken again to the coven and sexually abused.

"She took shower after shower all night long, Maddie. I almost believe it really happened, or something like it happened." Maddie told her she'd arranged for another series of counseling sessions with the therapist.

She checked on the progress of all the rest of her cases and by the end of the day she was ready to go home, eat, and see Rick.

He still wheeled himself around in the wheelchair from time to time, especially if it had been an especially grueling day with hours of exercise. He was in the wheelchair when Maddie walked in the door of her parents' home. The bruises on his face were virtually gone, she noticed, though he'd have scars there forever to remind him of his ordeal. Despite the scars, she still thought of him as handsome. The scars just gave him more character, more mystery, more mystique.

He grinned hugely when he saw her. "You're a sight for sore eyes!" he told her. "Guess what?"

"What?"

"I have permission to move back to my apartment and to drive again! Your mission, should you accept it, is to agree to come over and cook for me at night." He looked at her expectantly, hopefully.

"I'd be delighted to!" she answered, bending down to give him a kiss. "When will this happen?"

"Next week."

"Wonderful! Guess what! I've got some interesting news from work."

"What's that?"

"Remember the baby, Susie Q? The newborn that was left at the church back in November?"

"Yeah."

"Well, her parents came in this morning and want to try and get their baby back."

"Will they be able to?"

"They'll have to meet the judge's requirements, but they seem like a nice, intelligent young couple. He's got several scholarships to go to several different colleges in the fall and she's planning to work part-time and care for their baby."

Maddie got a fleeting wistful look in her eyes and Rick caught it before it was gone. He hesitated to ask her about it, however, knowing it probably had to do with the baby she lost and the horrific beating she endured in November which made sure she could never get pregnant again. If he and she ever got together, he'd suggest adoption to her because he wanted to have children around and highly suspected she did too.

"What's going on with Joe?" he asked.

"His trial has been set for March 5th. He's still claiming he did nothing wrong and thinks he can get away with all the beatings and attempted murders. We're all going to have to testify, you know. Gina, I heard, is looking forward to it. She plans to spare no details. Shirley, too."

"And you?"

Maddie looked at Rick and hesitated. "I guess I'm hoping I won't be called after my attorney calls Gina and Shirley and you."

"Your testimony is the most important one, Maddie," Rick told her quietly.

"But what he did to you was worse."

"No not really. He didn't castrate me to snuff out my manhood, like he hurt your ability to ever have children. Joe just wanted to get the three of us out of his way so he could get his hands on you. You're the key to his madness. Your testimony is essential to put him away."

Maddie lowered her head, heavy-hearted. She knew what Rick said was true but she got scared just thinking of sitting on the witness stand with him staring directly at her. She prayed earnestly that that could be avoided.

Rick reached for her chin and raised it, peering into her eyes with concern. "You can do it, Maddie. You have to. Otherwise he'll go free and come after you again."

"What about another protective order?"

"Did the first one work?"

"No," she answered sullenly.

Rick took a deep breath. "May I say something you probably don't want to hear?" She looked at him and slowly nodded. "First of all, you're not doing Joe any favors by simply forgiving him and pretending he didn't kill your baby or hurt you badly enough to make sure you never get pregnant again. Loving him and forgiving him is not the answer at this point. The man needs to be separated from the rest of society. He may be criminally insane, I don't know, I'm not a lawyer. But I do know he will not stop hunting you down and hurting you. Testifying is the only way to stop him, Maddie. He hurt your friend Gina to within an inch of her life and Officer Perkins to within an inch of hers. And he brutally raped and tortured you and left you to freeze to death in the cold. Then he did things to me no man should ever do to another man. Testifying against him is the only way to stop him from ever hurting anyone again."

Maddie was sobbing quieting through his recitation of Joe's actions against the people she cared about. She knew in her heart of heart he was right. She just felt like she would be betraying Joe by revealing everything he did to her. Then it dawned on her that Rick had said something about what Joe did to him and she looked up sharply at him.

"What did he do to you, Rick?" she asked. She was determined to learn what happened this time. He started to turn away, but she reached for his face and held it firmly, facing her. "Tell me, Rick. It's time I knew."

"Will it help you agree to testify?" he asked.

"Yes. I will testify if you tell me everything he did to you."

He nodded, clearly reluctant, but he had agreed. Looking down, he took a breath. "At first it was just one hell of a beating," he began. "He caught me unawares and had me knocked out before I knew it. Then he tied me down and when I woke he twisted my leg until it broke, then the same with my arm and broke the fingers on my hands, most of them anyway. He gagged me to keep the noise down. I passed out again and again but one time when I came to, he was naked and his dick was ready to play. He got me turned unto my stomach and-and he sodomized me. More than once. I passed out from all the pain again and when I woke up next, he was gone and I was half-clothed, still laying in the same place, some basement of a building. I managed to get myself untied somehow and crawled up the stairs to the outside, where I blacked out again. Someone must have found me and called the police." He stopped talking but couldn't look at Maddie. He felt ashamed of being bullied and beaten and sodomized without being able to ward the man off in the first place. Man, had he underestimated Joe's strength and determination!

"Rick? Look at me, please," Maddie said softly. He slowly raised his head and they saw the anguish in each other's eyes.

"I'm so sorry!" she told him tearfully. "I'm so very, very sorry that you had to go through that. It's all my fault!"

He leaned into her and encircled her with his arms. "I could say I'd do it again for you, Maddie, but I'd really rather not." She looked at him and surprised herself by laughing at the look on his face: earnest but seriously hoping she wouldn't ask him to. He smiled sadly. "Please testify against the man and put him away for good."

"I will, Rick. I won't hesitate anymore, I promise."

CHAPTER 13

Court Hearing

THE WEEKS FLEW BY. Rick got stronger but couldn't fully get rid of the weakness in his left leg. He had to resort to using a cane and walked with a decided limp. His left arm, likewise, had a weakness to it but the broken fingers had been rebroken and reset and were in the process of healing. All in all, he felt he had weathered the worst of the storm and was grateful he was on the way to full recovery.

Mentally, he geared up for the trial of Joe Skeeter which was fast approaching. He planned to mince no words and spare no details, despite the shame and embarrassment he felt at the brutal beating he had taken without getting in one lick of his own. He remembered how Joe made sure he was conscious whenever he caused the most pain and eagerly watched for him to black out over and over again, laughing at his power over Rick. Rick vaguely remembered Joe chortling whenever Rick screamed or tried in vain to avoid the painful blows, the twisting breaks of his leg and arm, the smashing of his fingers.

Rick shook himself to break the hold of the memories. But a smile slowly appeared on his face as he thought of Maddie. Not one word of disappointment escaped her lips about his inability to fight back, not one word of criticism for letting Joe sneak up on him unawares and do so much damage. Yet he continued to be confounded about how she could be so forgiving of the man after what he did to them. Unlike Maddie, his mind was full of bitter thoughts. He wanted to hurt Skeeter as badly as he'd been hurt, or worse. But then he took in a deep breath and tried to calm his mind. Physical revenge wasn't the answer, he knew that. But, he was positive that God wanted them both to tell the whole sordid truth of the terrible torment Skeeter had inflicted on them in a court of law. And he was ready!

That determination, as well as the fatigue from the therapy, stayed with him all the way home. Maddie had kept her promise to come and cook dinner for him each night and spend the evening with him. Her parents, whom he now called Lucy and Gary at their request, invited them over on Sundays for dinner after church. He still had six weeks of out-patient therapy to complete and he hoped by then that he could get rid of the cane.

As he sat down in his kitchen, Maddie arrived and he brightened immediately.

"Welcome to my abode," he said grinning. "How's your day been?"

"Fine. Filled with all those things CPS workers do during the day. How was yours?"

"Well, as you can tell I just finished therapy. I came straight home and I haven't showered yet. Can you sit tight for five minutes?"

"Sure." Maddie watched him limp over to the bathroom and close the door. She walked around his apartment looking for things to straighten up or to be dusted, but he was obsessive about neatness and there was nothing for her to do except sit down on the couch and wait for him. He emerged a few minutes later toweling his hair dry and sat down on the couch with her. Maddie admired his hair; it had such a nice, natural wave to it.

"Are you ready for the hearing next week?" he asked her.

"Yes, I've been meeting with my lawyer, Caitlin Patterson, and she's given me pointers on how to dress, to be polite even if the other attorney is rude or demeaning, to be truthful, to answer all the questions put to me, etc. She's determined to do her best for us and put Joe away for as long as possible. This is a lady you wouldn't want to tangle with, Rick. At least not verbally. Maybe not physically, either. She's tall, strong, and fights to win."

Rick grinned at the description and thought: another battleax like Gina, Perkins and Claymore to deal with. But Patterson's battlefield was in the courtroom and her armor, so to speak, was her command of the law and the English language while she stood toe to toe with Joe's attorney and did her best to beat the pants off him. He chuckled. They needed someone like her, while at the same time, he wondered about Skeeter's attorney. Was it a female taken in by his false charm or a man sticking up for one of his own kind, maybe with a grudge against women himself? He had a hard time imagining anyone working his butt off for Skeeter. But, he reminded himself as he'd reminded Maddie earlier, everyone deserves a defense.

"She's going to meet with you, too, Rick," said Maddie, interrupting his reverie, "and go over your testimony."

He nodded. "Are you ready to tell the judge and jury everything Joe did to you?" he asked her. She nodded.

"But, I don't understand why he's going through with this trial, Rick. He can't win, not with Gina and Shirley's testimonies, plus mine and yours. He must know that! I can't understand why his attorney doesn't try to talk him out of it."

"Because he deserves a fair hearing, too, Maddie. He's technically not guilty until the judge and jury say so. And, like it or not, he deserves a good defense."

Maddie made a face at him but she knew that he was right. She just didn't want to go through the humiliation of testifying about what he did to her. Truth be told, she didn't want Rick to know all the details. What if he decided she was damaged goods after hearing everything, that she was undesirable? Of course, he went through much the same ordeal and in no way did she think of him as damaged goods. But that was different. She loved him and would love him no matter how badly he was hurt. In fact, her love for him was growing exponentially. Her prayer was that his love for her was growing, too. What a couple they would make, though! Him limping around, his fingers still healing; her unable to bear him any children. Kind of sad, actually.

She shook the thoughts away and forced a big smile for Rick. "Well, Tiger, ready for dinner?"

"You bet! I'm famished. What're you going to make tonight?"

"Spaghetti okay?"

"Super! You don't always have to cook, though, you know. I like take-out and good old-fashioned hamburgers, too."

"Now you tell me!" she teased, "after I've been cooking for you all this time!"

"But I like your cooking," he protested. "I like it better than take-out, but I just don't want to burden you with it every night." Maddie planted a kiss on his lips to shush him and went to make the spaghetti sauce. During the meal, they talked about the upcoming trial and tried to bolster each other's spirits.

The trial began with jury selection. When Caitlin Patterson and the opposing counsel, Ross Jenkins, were satisfied with the twelve jurors selected, the opening statements began.

Caitlin was up first. She strode confidently toward the jury and took a moment to look each one in the eyes.

"Friends," she said, "what I'm about to say to you will be difficult to hear. You are going to learn about the horrific things that Joseph Skeeter did to Madison Roper while she was his wife and then even more horrific things that he did to her on November 21st, eighteen months after their divorce.

"I will show that, without a shadow of a doubt, Joseph Skeeter deliberately and knowingly beat Madison Roper while they were still married and living in Pueblo, Colorado, knocking her down and kicking her repeatedly in the stomach, causing her to lose their baby. She left him that night and returned to Colorado Springs, to her parents. On the way up here, she began hemorrhaging and as soon as she arrived, was rushed to the hospital where the baby perished. As soon as she was able, she divorced Mr. Skeeter and was issued a protective order against him.

"Eighteen months later, Joseph Skeeter located Ms. Roper up here and tried to make contact with her, despite the protective order meant to prevent that from happening. Ms. Roper's boss, Janie Cosgrove, assigned another worker from Child Protective Services, Ms. Gina Martinez, to go everywhere with her in case Mr. Skeeter tried anything. Mr. Skeeter wasted no time in attacking Ms. Martinez and choking her to within an inch of her life. The police then assigned Officer Shirley Perkins as Ms. Roper's bodyguard, but Mr. Skeeter snuck up on her in her car and whacked her on the head, causing a severe concussion. At that point, he kidnapped Ms. Roper and drove up into the mountains. You will hear Ms. Roper's testimony of how he beat her without mercy, how he raped her over and over, how he ripped her insides apart, making it impossible for her to ever have any children again. Then," said Caitlin Patterson, lowering her voice so that the jurors had to lean forward to hear her, "she will testify that he left her out on the ground up on that mountain road, in freezing weather, with no clothes on, and miles away from help. Only by the grace of God," she went on, louder, "did someone happen to come along that deserted road and see her lying on the ground and call the police. Only by the grace of God did they get there in time to save her life.

"But, my friends, Joe Skeeter wasn't done yet causing havoc and inflicting pain," she went on, drawing the jurors in with her eyes. "He grabbed Ms. Roper's good friend, Rick Shelby, another Child Protection worker, and Mr. Shelby will testify that Joseph Skeeter proceeded to knock him out, drag him down to the basement of an abandoned building, tie him down, and beat him unconscious. Then Mr. Skeeter took great pleasure in twisting and breaking Mr. Shelby's left leg in several places, and his left arm and the fingers on both of his hands. Mr. Shelby will also testify that Mr. Skeeter then sodomized him repeatedly and ultimately left him still tied up and close to death. Again, only by the grace of God was Mr. Shelby able to get himself untied enough to crawl up the steps from that basement room to the outside. And, mercifully, by the grace of God, someone saw him and called the police."

Caitlin took a breath and studied the jurors for a moment. "Listen well to the doctors' reports, the expert witnesses, and the victims themselves: Ms. Gina Martinez, Officer Shirley Perkins, Mr. Rick Shelby, and Ms. Madison Roper," she urged. "They will tell you the truth about what Joseph Skeeter did to them. You will come to believe, as I do, that Joseph Skeeter does not belong in civilized society but in a prison far away where he cannot hurt anyone again. Thank you."

Judge Kohlenberg called a noon-time recess and in moments the courtroom was empty. Once back in the courtroom, Joe's attorney, Mr. Ross Jenkins, began by stating that in spite of the horrific allegations against his client, he would prove that they were nothing more than exaggerations and downright lies, that Mr. Skeeter was not capable of causing such harm to anybody.

Jenkins stated, "Mr. Skeeter's actions were misunderstood. When he and his wife were together, he was only pleading with her not to leave him when she accidently fell and injured herself in the stomach, enough to lose her baby. Then she left in the middle of the night, leaving no note saying where she was going or why she was leaving him. He hunted for her for over a year, and, yes when he found her he tried to make contact with her, despite the protective order. He yearned for his wife, you can understand that. He loved her. He still loves her and is willing to forgive her for putting him through this terrible ordeal." He droned on in his mesmerizing voice and Maddie saw that some of the jurors were getting confused about who to believe.

She sat in stunned silence. She wanted to stand up and scream at Jenkins that none of that was true, but Caitlin took her hand and squeezed it and she was able to calm down. She watched Caitlin listening carefully to Jenkins, jotting down notes and questions for herself.

When Jenkins was finished, the judge asked Caitlin to call her first witness. She called Pastor Gary Roper to the stand to tell about the morning Maddie had returned home from Pueblo after being beaten and kicked by her husband. Roper described how she was already hemorrhaging, in fact was covered in blood from the waist down, and they barely had time to greet her before rushing her to the hospital where she lost her baby.

Caitlin then brought in the doctor who attended Maddie on that occasion, Dr. Fritz Heinrich, who reported upon the damage done to Maddie's uterus by the kicking she received. He reported bruises from Skeeter's boots all over her stomach, arms, and breasts, and that her fall was not an accident. He spoke clearly and slowly because of his German accent. He was very convincing.

Caitlin then called Maddie to the stand to relate her story. She led her gently through her ordeal in Pueblo, making sure she left out no detail of importance. Maddie endured the questioning but lost control and cried on a couple of occasions. The judge was kind and provided a tissue box for her.

When Caitlin was finished questioning her, Jenkins got up and slowly approached the witness stand. "Ms. Roper, or should I say Mrs. Skeeter, which is your married name, correct?"

"It was, but when I divorced Joe I change my name back to my maiden name, Madison Roper. Please address me as Ms. Roper." Her reply caused Jenkins to pause momentarily but he quickly recovered. "Of course, if that's what you would like. But, tell me, why did you marry Joe Skeeter in the first place? Didn't you love him?"

"I did, in the beginning."

"And now? Don't you still love him? After all you gave him four years of your life."

Maddie thought about how to answer that, then said, "I love him as a person, sir, just as I love all people."

"But you don't love him enough to stay married to him or return to him?"

"No, I don't.

"Tell me, Ms. Roper, why do you say he beat you up back when you two were still married and living together back in Pueblo?"

"Why? Because he did."

"What exactly makes you say that? You tripped and fell, hitting your stomach, correct?

"No, that's not correct, Mr. Jenkins."

"Well, what exactly did happen, Ms. Roper, in you opinion—and remember, you're under oath."

Collecting herself, she said, "First, he came home very late and very drunk. I'd been waiting up to tell him the good news that we were going to have a baby."

"Did you tell him?"

"Yes, I did."

"And then what happened, according to you?"

Hiding her anger at his insinuations, she kept her voice calm and replied, "He slapped me across the face, then backhanded me, knocking me down to the floor."

"Are you sure you didn't just trip?"

"No, I did not trip."

"Okay, whatever. You find yourself on the floor. What do you do next?"

"I skootched away from him because he was coming toward me in a menacing way, anger in his eyes. I bumped up against the wall and couldn't go any farther."

"And then?" Maddie couldn't believe he was making her spell everything out so clearly. How was he going to refute it?

"And then he proceeded to kick me in the stomach," she said, staring him straight in the eyes. "He kicked me over and over, Mr. Jenkins. I drew myself into a ball to protect the baby and waited it out. When he finally stopped, he went over to the couch, as usual, and passed out. I waited until I could hear him snoring, then I got up and got out of there. I drove straight up here to my parents' home and, on the way, I could feel the blood already running down my legs and seeping into my clothes. By the time I arrived, I was covered in blood from the waist down. I was afraid I'd pass out before I made it home. I prayed for strength."

Jenkins blinked a couple of times, then he scoffed slightly. "You have quite an imagination, Ms. Roper. "That's all an exaggeration, right? It wasn't quite like that, was it? You tripped and fell, hitting your stomach in the process. I understand you lost your baby, but blaming it on your loving husband? That's pretty cold! No further questions."

The judge called a recess.

Caitlin, Rick and the Ropers did their best to calm Maddie down, who was crying from Jenkins' cruel cross-examination.

"You did wonderful," Caitlin told her soothingly. "And Jenkins knew you did. Now, brace yourself, Maddie. Tomorrow we'll be dealing with the November assault when we go in there. Put on a brave face."

The next morning, Caitlin called Gina Martinez first to give her testimony, then Officer Perkins, then the man who saw her lying naked on the side of the deserted mountain road and called the cops, then the cops and EMTs who found her and covered her up with their coats, gave her oxygen and rushed her to the hospital, and then Dr. Benjamin Marshall who treated her in the emergency room. Finally she called Dr. Arnold Flowers, who performed the surgery to stop the bleeding and repair as much of the damage done to her uterus and ovaries as possible.

"She will never be able to get pregnant and bear a child again," he reported solemnly, sadly.

Jenkins did his best to discredit the many eye witnesses, minimize their damaging testimonies, and paint a softer, gentler picture of the defendant. Skeeter, for his part, sat and glared at every witness who took the stand. Maddie feared he would try to retaliate somehow.

Caitlin's final witness was Rick Shelby. She had him report about Skeeter stalking them, assaulting them at the restaurant, and then his ordeal when Skeeter took him and nearly killed him. True to his word, Rick told every detail he could remember of what the man did to him and stared at Skeeter the whole time he was on the stand. Skeeter blinked first.

Jenkins got up and approached Rick. "Mr. Shelby, would you say you're in love with Ms. Roper and that you hate Mr. Skeeter because he interfered with your amorous intentions?"

Rick answered carefully, "Yes, I love Madison Roper, but no, I do not hate Joe Skeeter. I hate what he did to her. I am appalled—."

"So, you do hate him."

"No, I said I hate what he did to Ms. Roper. There's a difference."

"Come on, Mr. Shelby. That's hogwash. You hate him. Say it. You wish he were dead."

"No, I won't say that, Mr. Jenkins! But I do wish for justice for Ms. Roper."

"But not for yourself?" Jenkins scoffed. "You don't want justice for yourself, Mr. Shelby?"

"I survived. I'll heal. But Ms. Roper will never be able to bear children again because of Joe Skeeter. That's unforgiveable."

Jenkins huffed and turned away. "No further questions, Your Honor," he said and sat down.

Caitlin had no more witnesses and rested.

Jenkins had few witnesses to put on the stand in Joe's defense. He minimized that by saying they were afraid to come forward for fear Ms. Roper would come after them and retaliate. Caitlin rebutted by putting Janie Cosgrove and Joan Perez on the stand as character witnesses, who portrayed Maddie as the kind, caring person she was and testified that she put up with Joe for as long as she did because she loved him. Jenkins declined to question the character witnesses, acting as if they were not important enough to bother with.

The next morning, Caitlin got up to present her closing argument. She reiterated much of what she had said in the beginning and, to Maddie's ears, she was convincing. Jenkins closing statement held few surprises and Maddie was relieved when he was done.

Judge Kohlenberg carefully instructed the jurors on their duties and reminded them that their decision had to be unanimous. The charges against Joe included one count of aggravated assault, one count of assault of a police officer, two counts of rape, and four counts of attempted murder.

While the jury was out deliberating, Caitlin, Rick, Maddie, and the Ropers went to a nearby coffeeshop to have a cup of coffee.

"Now we wait," said Caitlin, but she was smiling broadly. They all looked at her eagerly. "I have a good feeling, folks. We have a strong case," she stated.

Forty-five minutes later, the call came that the jury had reached a verdict. They hurried back over to the courthouse. Maddie couldn't tell if reaching a verdict that quickly was a good sign or not. Taking their seats, the courtroom abuzz with whispers, the bailiff finally told everyone to rise and a hush fell as Judge Kohlenberg entered and took the bench. Everyone sat, full of anticipation.

The jurors then filed in and the judge asked if they had reached a verdict. The lead juror stood up and said that they had.

The bailiff took the paper with the verdict on it over to the judge who read it silently and handed it back to the bailiff to return it to the juror.

"Will the defendant please rise," intoned the judge. Jenkins rose and had to pull Skeeter to his feet.

Then the judge said to the lead juror, "Please read the verdict aloud."

"We find the defendant guilty of all charges," the man said, looking over at Skeeter without blinking. "We find him guilty of one count of aggravated assault, one count of assault of a police officer, two counts of rape, and four counts of attempted murder." The juror returned the paper to the bailiff and sat down.

Joe Skeeter stared at the juror, dumbfounded, the color draining from his face. "No!" he shouted. "You're wrong! I wasn't trying to hurt my wife or anyone else! I just wanted my wife back!" Two officers came forward immediately to restrain him but he pushed them away and turned toward Maddie and tried to reach for her. Two more officers came forward to help. In the melee, people in the front rows of the courtroom scattered out of the way. Joe started throwing punches, knocking one officer down in the process. More officers came rushing forward, and Joe suddenly found himself in shackles. He bellowed and hollered and swore, but five officers had a firm grip on him and were forcibly escorting him out of the courtroom.

"Maddie!" he cried, a wildness in his eyes, "Maddie! I only want you to come back to me! Please! Just come back!" The next minute he was gone from the courtroom.

Maddie started shaking. Rick wrapped his arms around her and she buried her head in his shoulder. Her parents hovered close at hand, as did Caitlin. Everyone was ready to protect her should Joe somehow get away from the officers and come charging back in. As peace reigned again in the room, however, everyone began to relax. Maddie let out the breath she'd been holding.

They stayed put until the bailiff returned and let them know it was safe to leave.

CHAPTER 15

Sentencing

OUTSIDE THE COURTROOM, MADDIE got separated from her parents, but Rick was still by her side. She found herself surrounded by news reporters, their cameras flashing, and all of them yelling rapid-fire questions at her. Caitlin pushed them out of the way, reminding Rick of a football player with her arm outstretched and hustled them toward the elevators.

"No comment at this time!" Caitlin repeated over and over. "Give the lady have some breathing space!"

Finally they were outside at Caitlin's car. Maddie and Rick tried to hurry Maddie inside it since the reporters were already streaming out of the courthouse and heading straight for them.

"Get in the car," ordered Caitlin, and Rick virtually shoved Maddie inside, then got in himself. Caitlin joined them and locked the doors, started the car, and drove off. "Where do you want me to take you?" she asked.

"To the Ropers' home," answered Rick.

Maddie finally got control of herself, stopped shaking and turned to Caitlin. "Thank you so much!" she said. "You were so good in there!"

"There's still the sentencing phase to get through, you know. We'll meet and talk about that at another time."

"What kind of sentence could he get?" asked Maddie, not wanting to put it off.

"He could potentially get 48 years to life, whatever the judge deems appropriate for the charges against him. Whatever it turns out to be, he'll be an old man by the time he gets out of prison, Maddie. So, you're basically free now to live your life as you see fit without worrying about Skeeter showing up again to bother you." Caitlin smiled at Maddie. "These are the kinds of cases I live for," she said. "Men like Skeeter don't belong out in the world hurting decent people. When you get home you two, relax, and do me a favor. Have a drink on me." She pulled in front of the parsonage and kissed Maddie on the cheek. Good luck with the rest of your life, Maddie. You, too, Rick."

As Rick and Maddie entered the parsonage, they found it empty.

"I hope they didn't get mobbed by the reporters," said Maddie.

"I have no doubt your father will do just fine with them. He's got the gift of gab. They'll probably all show up for services on Sunday after he's done with them." Maddie chuckled and wrapped her arms around Rick's neck.

"Thank you for your wonderful testimony up there. You really didn't mince any words. I was so proud of you."

"Yeah, well, you didn't do so badly yourself, you know."

The Ropers arrived several minutes later, talking excitedly about the hearing. Then, grinning from ear to ear, Roper proudly admitted to giving the reporters a brief statement. Lucy, Maddie and Rick applauded him and he took a bow. But then the enormity of the hearing and what had been accomplished hit them and they collapsed as one in the living room to catch their breath.

At they sat in silence. Lucy got up and headed for the kitchen. Ever the hostess, she returned with a tray of coffee and brownies for them to munch on while they sorted out their thoughts and feelings. All eyes were on Maddie who barely touched her brownie, just stared off into space.

Finally she looked at everyone. "I feel so bad for Joe," she said. "He's going to rot in prison for the rest of his life for what he did. We all lived through the assaults, so why does he have to be punished so harshly?"

Rick took her hand and Roper joined them on the couch.

"Let me put it this way," said Rick. "We lived through our assaults because: one, we were all strong and healthy, not because he wanted us to. Two, kind people came to our rescue. And three, God was watching over us. We didn't survive because of Joe, believe me, because he couldn't have cared less if Gina, Shirley or I made it through. But I believe, from the depths of my soul, that he wanted you to die, Maddie. If he couldn't have you, nobody else was either. He may even have thought that if you did survive the freezing weather with no clothes, badly injured and bleeding, stranded on a barren mountain road seldom traveled by anyone, that you'd be so damaged no man would want you even if you did survive." Rick paused to swallow his rage at Skeeter. "He deserves the punishment he gets," he ended.

Pastor Roper cleared his throat. "I believe the Good Lord was looking out for you, Mads. Like Rick, I also believe that Joe did not mean for you to survive. He left you to die. A decent person would have felt remorse. A decent person would have returned to help you or called and got help for you. But Joe did neither. Face it, Mads, Joe is exactly where he belongs, locked up and unable to hurt you or Rick or anyone else ever again."

"Okay," said Lucy with forced brightness. "Mads, please eat the delicious brownie I made for you so I'll feel better."

Looking up at her in surprise, she could see that her mother was close to falling apart.

"Come on, Mads," coaxed her father but Maddie shook her head no. Her stomach wasn't up to it at the moment.

"If you'll excuse me," she said rising from the couch. "I just want to be alone for a while," and she headed up the stairs to her old room and since there was no bed there any longer, she laid down on the floor.

Lucy sat where Maddie had been and the three worried about Maddie in silence as they ate their brownie and drank their coffee.

At the sentencing hearing, Skeeter was subdued, barely looking at Maddie, and stood to hear the judge's verdict without prodding. Judge Kohlenberg spoke gravely as he sentenced him to the maximum amount of sentence: life in prison with no parole.

"I'll appeal!" Skeeter immediately yelled at the judge. Jenkins tried to quiet him down, warning him not to create any more disturbance. He was clearly tired of his client's behavior.

Joe then turned to Maddie and glared at her with such hatred she cringed and backed as far away from him as she could get.

"And you!" he yelled threateningly, finger thrusting in her direction. "I'll get even with you one way or the other! You won't even see me coming! I'll kill you, you bitch! But you'll suffer before you'll die! You'll beg me to let you die!" Officers rushed rapidly over to him, shackled him and forcibly escorted him out, cutting off his tirade.

Maddie started shaking again. Rick wrapped his arms around her and gently coaxed her out of the courtroom. Caitlin moved people out of the way so they could get to the elevator. On the first floor, she led them into a small meeting room and closed the door. Rick held Maddie close, trying to calm her down. With great effort, she pulled herself together.

"I'm sorry for going to pieces," she apologized, drying her eyes.

"You're safe now, Maddie," said Rick and Caitlin together. Caitlin went on, "Should he ever get released, say for good behavior—which is hard to imagine—he'd be so old he probably won't even remember what he said. You're going to be just fine, Maddie, I promise."

Maddie smiled gratefully at her attorney and Rick. "Thank you, both of you," she murmured. Then, taking a deep breath she stood to let them know she had pulled herself together. Caitlin let out a sigh of relief.

At the Roper house, Maddie was surprised by the crowd of people in the living room: Janie, Joan and Gene among them, plus many others from work and church. They greeted her with heartfelt hugs. All were there to congratulate her and the only topic of conversation was the hearing and sentencing. Maddie plastered a smile on her face and endured it. She didn't want to think about Joe or talk about the hearing anymore. She just wanted to get used to the indisputable fact that he would not be around to hurt her or Rick anymore. She was eager to get back to work and her old routine.

But later that evening as she crawled wearily into bed, she wondered what to do about Rick. He'd been such an angel throughout the whole ordeal, not to mention going through what he went through, too. He was so sweet, so kind and caring. He was everything she wanted in a husband. But what could she give him? Nothing. No children and maybe not even lovemaking. She was so damaged. He deserved so much better than that.

She loved him with all her heart and over the past few weeks he had made it abundantly clear that he loved her as well. He even said so in court while up on the stand. A smile lit up her face as she remembered. Sweet, adorable Rick, scars and all. He deserved someone who wasn't as damaged as her. He deserved a whole, healthy woman who could make love to him and bear him children. That started her thinking of women who could love Rick properly. There was Joan from church, a happy, God-fearing woman who'd lost her husband shortly after they were married. She was their age and lonely and already half in love with Rick. Then she thought of Monica Tubbs at CPS and started giggling. Monica never did forgive him for taking over at the Durant home visit on his first day. Nope, not Monica. How about Yoli Blanco at work? A striking Latina, vivacious and energetic. She'd keep Rick happy in bed, no doubt about it. Or Darla Yin, a beautiful Oriental woman with a deep love for children.

As her eyes drifted closed, the smile left her face and tears started running down her cheeks. She didn't want to give Rick up to someone else. But how could she make him happy when she had nothing to offer him?

Back at Child Protective Services full-time again, Maddie got back into the routine of home visits, court hearings, meetings, and permanency plans. She immersed herself, happy to deal with other peoples' problems instead of her own. The last doctor visit she'd gone to revealed she had healed as much as she was going to from her injuries, at least physically. Emotionally? She wasn't sure how long that would take. She found herself still having flashbacks and nightmares about up in the mountains and would start shivering as if freezing all over again. How grateful she felt to the man who had driven up that road and saw her and took the time to make the call to the police. How grateful she was to the EMTs who saved her life that day. Stop it! Time to think about cases, the Durants and the Ordmans and Susie Q, and to quit thinking about Joe and what he did.

She remembered seeing the Durant family in church on Sunday, looking happy together. That brought a smile to her face. The case had already been closed after Durant had apologized to Dawn. Fortunately, Dawn did not get pregnant from the rape. The Ordmans were also doing fine. Clarissa reported no new beatings and said her mom was being nicer to her when she did her hair. As for Susie Q, Maddie wondered how that case was coming along. Were Roni and Neal able to get the baby back? Curious, Maddie headed for Janie's office to find out.

"I'm happy to report," said Janie, "that Roni and Neal have gotten married, that Neal has a full scholarship to the University of Colorado, that they've secured an apartment with the help of Neal's parents, and that they have a court date next week to get their baby back. I'm really proud of them, Maddie."

"Me, too!"

The next day Roni and Neal came into the office, Maddie went out to meet with them. She gave them both a hug. "I wish you all the luck in the world at your hearing. I hope you get Susie Q back."

"Thank you," grinned Roni. "We've chosen a new name for her—not that there's anything wrong with Susie Q—but we wanted to name her after Neal's grandmother."

"Wonderful! What will her new name be?"

"Melora. Melora Janis Jefferson. She's so beautiful, Maddie! Her foster mom, Doris, has done a wonderful job of caring for her, but I'm ready to take over and be her mother now."

"You're going to be a great mother, Roni, I know it! And you, Neal, a full scholarship to the University of Colorado! That's wonderful! I'm so proud of the both of you! When you get your baby back, if there's anything I can do to help, please let me know. Melora has a special place in my heart since I found her in that blanket outside the church door."

Roni and Neal looked at each other then back at Maddie.

"There is one thing," said Roni, grinning hopefully. "We'd like you to be Melora's godmother."

Maddie was stunned. "Oh my! Why, I'd be honored!"

"Great! We're going to be joining your church soon and we'll have Melora baptized at the same time. By the way," she said, lowing her voice conspiratorially, I heard you're going with Rick Shelby from your church. Are you two going to get married, because we'd like him to be the godfather."

Maddie wasn't sure how to answer since she had made up her mind not to marry Rick after all. She settled on telling them they could ask him to be Melora's godfather whether they married or not.

"But he loves you, Maddie. I overheard him talking with one of the other workers here, Jaime. Rick's so cute, he's perfect for you." Not sure what to say to that, Maddie settled for simply hugging the two young people and gracefully made her exit.

Back in her office, she sat and pondered the situation, befuddled all over again about what to do with Rick. She had been trying to avoid him since the trial ended in an effort to build some distance between them. But he was such a wonderful person, she would truly love to marry him. If only she didn't feel so strongly that he deserved someone better than her. Someone who could give him children.

Pushing thoughts of Rick aside, she went back to reviewing her cases. After checking on Roni and Neal's hearing date, she put it in her calendar so she could attend. It was just two weeks away.

When their hearing came due, she planted herself in the courtroom to listen to the judge's decision. Their caseworker, Margy Dormstetter, did an excellent job of reviewing their progress and excellent parent-child visits, and highly recommended Susie Q, who would be renamed officially as Melora, be returned to the young parents, with follow-up visits for six weeks. Judge Howard Conklin, the CPS judge, was duly impressed with the worker's report and granted the child to be returned to his parents.

Margy happily congratulated them and wished them well. Roni said they were going to call Pastor Roper right away and set a date for them to join the church and for Melora to be baptized.

"Oh," said Roni, "I asked Rick to be the godfather and he agreed. You've got to marry him, Margy, before he gets away!" With that, Roni kissed her on the cheek and she and Neal headed over to Maggy to collect their baby and all the belongings she'd accumulated during the past six months. Maddie watched them go with a big smile on her face. Melora, she thought. What a pretty name.

Two weeks later, Roni and Neal Jefferson were taken in as new members of the church during the morning worship service and Melora was baptized. Maddie and Rick stood up as godparents for the child.

Following the service, Rick tried to get Maddie aside to talk with her, but she seemed to find things to do and people to see, making it difficult if not impossible. He joined her at the Ropers, as usual, for Sunday dinner, but again, she stayed busy and out of his way. He left with the distinct feeling that she was deliberately avoiding him. He vowed to keep trying until he wore her down enough for her to sit still and hear him out.

Maddie was fully aware of Rick pursuing her and kept devising ways to avoid him because she knew if she was face to face with him and looking in those eyes of his, she would lose track of her senses. She had to find a way to help him see the advantage of dating Joan or Yoli or Darla and forget about her. But how to go about that? He already crossed paths with the women on a regular basis. How could she improve their odds with him? Surprisingly, a thought occurred to her: double-dating. She'd find someone to take her out and invite Rick and one of the three to go out with them. Of course, he'd be awfully confused and she could picture the look on his face as he tried to figure out what she was up to, causing her to giggle. On the other hand, knowing Rick, he'd figure it out so fast the whole idea would blow up and chase the eligible women away.

Sigh.

What to do?

She was ready to give up on the idea and just continue to avoid Rick as much as possible until he eventually got the message and drifted away, finding someone else on his own. But that thought caused a pain deep in her heart and she broke down and cried. There was no good answer for the dilemma she was in.

Monday morning, Maddie arrived at work and was determined to direct all her energy into visiting her foster children, testifying in court on their behalf, and writing her reports. This will be my life from now on, she told herself. I need to make the most of it. I will love my foster children as if they were my own and not think about marriage or Rick. I will stay busy here and at church. I will forget about Joe and all the pain he caused. Instead, I will praise God for the blessings I do have and not cry over what I don't have. But, Oh, Lord, help Rick understand. He knows I'm avoiding him. Please help him to accept my decision.

CHAPTER 15

Rick's Determination

IN THE MIDDLE OF her befuddled contemplation as she tried in vain to work on a permanency plan for a new case, Rick appeared at her door. She looked up with a start and immediately felt trapped. And guilty. There was no way to avoid him now. He leaned on his cane momentarily and studied her, a firm set to his mouth. She soaked in his renewed strength and well-being. The months of therapy had paid off. He was almost back to his old self and all her resolve to avoid him fled out the window. She had missed his hugs and kisses so much! But, there was no way they could have a future together. She wouldn't burden him with that. But, oh, how she longed for him to hold her.

"Hi, Rick," she said timidly, trying to smile without looking guilty for avoiding him. Now what was she supposed to do with him standing right there studying her so intently? Keep typing and ignore him?

"We need to talk," he said into the awkward silence and she saw the determination in his eyes.

"About what?" she asked innocently, hoping he meant about a case and not about them.

"We need to talk about us," he replied, eyes riveted on Maddie. Without taking his eyes off her, as if he was afraid she'd disappear if he did, he reached behind himself and closed her door, then sat down in her visitor's chair.

"Us?" she asked. Just the word made her heart pound. This was exactly what she wanted to avoid, especially those eyes of his which could be so intense. Like now.

"Yes! Ever since the trial ended, you've been avoiding me. I'd like to know why." Maddie flushed a bright color and looked down to break the hold of his eyes. "Talk to me, Maddie," he said more quietly, realizing he was coming on a little too strong. "Have I done something to offend you or hurt you?" She shook her head no. "Then what's going on?"

"It's me, Rick," she said, afraid to look up, her eyes filling with tears. "It's all me! It's my fault. You've done nothing wrong." But then she didn't know how to proceed. Rick sat there waiting for her to continue but when she didn't, he started to say what he guessed was on her mind. But before he could, she blurted out in an anguished voice, "You deserve someone whole and healthy, Rick! You deserve someone who can-who can give you what you want and need in life! Like a healthy marriage with sex and children. I can't do either of those things anymore."

He scooted his chair closer and took her hands firmly in his. She couldn't pull away; plus the warmth of his hands felt so good. He was trembling slightly, still intense. She felt his soaring emotions like electricity tingling her fingers.

"Maddie, I love you! Don't you understand? I love you just the way you are! Would I be hanging around and pestering you all the time if I didn't? I want to marry you, Maddie! We'll find a way to be sexual, but more importantly we'll love each other and adopt children and make a home, a family! I just want us to be together for the rest of our lives." She began to sob silently, head bowed. But Rick would have none of that and lifted her chin. "Look at me, Maddie."

Her eyes brimmed with tears as she met his gaze.

"I know you love me, Maddie," he continued softly. "I feel it and I see it in your eyes. We can make a life together in spite of what Joe did to us. We're both damaged goods, if you want to look at it that way. But, sweetheart, we can't let that ruin the rest of our lives. You deserve happiness and love and I want to be the one to give it to you."

Maddie's eyes softened but the flow of tears increased. "I'm a mess, Rick," she said. "I'm not sure I can even make love anymore, he hurt me so badly. You deserve someone better, someone whole and healthy." The words she been afraid to say finally came out and she waited for his reaction. Her heart, she found, wasn't as convinced of the truth of those words as it had been earlier. Not with him sitting right there so close and looking at her so lovingly. His words, his love felt like a spring shower falling on her, turning her dry, withered life into one of love and hope and promise.

Rick pulled her chair as close to him as possible and leaned forward to give her a kiss. "That's the last time you think or say those words, Maddie," he told her. "I love you and I want to marry you. No one else. I understand all the medical stuff you're referring to, but I. Love. You. Anyway! I want you to be my wife."

Maddie's heart finally began to dance. She was crying harder but now they were tears of happiness. "Oh, Rick!" she whispered, "I was so afraid to hope that you. . ."

"Shh." He leaned forward and kissed her soundly to stop her words.

Of course, someone had to knock and open the door at that point. "Oh!" came the surprised exclamation. "I'm sorry!" It was Jaime and he hurriedly closed the door and left. Rick and Maddie both sat back abruptly and broke up laughing.

"It's going to be all over the building in one second," predicted Rick, still clinging to Maddie. "Are we okay now?" he asked her. She nodded with joy, a big smile on her face in spite of the tears. "Good, because I want to properly propose to you, but I had to clear the air first. However, right now I guess we better open the door and face the music out there," he said, standing up and pushing his chair back in its proper place.

When Rick, still clinging to Maddie's hand like he'd never let go again, opened her door the hallway was full of workers watching for them to emerge, who immediately started clapping and hooting with joy. Rick and Maddie stood close together and grinned at them.

"When's the wedding?" someone called and everyone approached them and started shaking Rick's hand and hugging Maddie. Janie came out of her office to see what the fuss was all about and Jaime quickly filled her in. Janie beamed.

"Congratulations you two!" she said and gave them both a strong hug. "How about we all go out to lunch? Then they can tell us all about it."

Cheers went up from the crowd. Members of other teams wanted to go also so that there were close to fifteen workers in all plus Janie who arrived at the restaurant. The staff hurried to pull some tables together to accommodate the group. Once settled, Janie called for everyone to hush and asked Rick and Maddie to fill them in on what was happening.

So Rick did.

"But," he said, "before Maddie could say yes to my proposal, we were interrupted by an intruder." Rick cleared his throat and looked directly at Jaime, then grinned and went on, "So I'd like to take this opportunity now to ask her properly. With your permission, of course," he said to everyone and they cheered him on. He knew he was taking a risk—Maddie could say no—but he was willing to take that chance.

A hush fell as Rick turned to Maddie, took out his handkerchief from his pocket, laid it on the floor, and knelt on it. Peering hopefully, lovingly up into her face, he spoke the traditional words: "Madison Roper, will you marry me?" He then held his breath.

"Yes!" she answered breathlessly.

Cheers went up around the table, along with hoots and hollers from other customers who had been watching their table with interest. They added their clapping and well-wishes. A bottle of Sangria miraculously appeared on the table and the waiter produced small glasses so everyone could toast the newly engaged couple.

"Where's the ring?" called Jaime.

"Still at the jewelry store. I was just paving the way today. She'll have the ring tomorrow."

The rest of the luncheon was filled with bantering, teasing, and well-wishes. By the time they got back to the office, the whole building knew of the engagement and the rest of the day seemed more like a celebration than a work day.

Rick followed her to the Ropers' house to break the good news to them. They were hugged and kissed and congratulated and it was unanimously decided that they would go out for a nice meal at a fancy restaurant to celebrate.

Afterwards, Gary Roper took Rick aside while the ladies were still in the restroom. "Are you okay with Mads not being able to give you any children?"

"I told her we could adopt. I know she loves kids; so do I, for that matter. Whatever she wants is what we'll do, Gary. I want her to be happy."

Gary beamed at him. "Thank you for being the kind of man you are, Rick. We will be so proud to have you for a son-in-law." Roper was clapping Rick on the shoulder as the women returned from the restroom.

That evening at Maddie's apartment, they sat and talked for a long time, Rick reassuring her over and over that everything would be alright, that he loved her totally and did not consider her damaged or diminished in any way. Maddie had a hard time fully understanding that he could feel that way but the joy in her heart was sufficient for the time being. She only knew that she loved Rick totally, that he was the man she wanted to marry, and that she was ecstatic he had confronted her that morning and cleared the air. She thanked God over and over that night for granting her this chance at happiness. As for children? They would definitely adopt!

The next day, Rick and Maddie headed for the jewelers to pick out an engagement ring and wedding bands. Joan offered to cook them a nice dinner and bring it to Maddie's apartment, serve them and then disappear. She had everything in readiness when they arrived, including candles on the table, flowers, cloth napkins, and good china. Joan had made them chicken cordon bleu, asparagus with Hollandaise sauce, and baked potatoes. She had also baked a strawberry-rhubarb pie for dessert.

True to her word, when they were seated at the table she served them and then quietly departed.

"She's a special friend," noted Rick.

"I'm going to ask her to be my matron of honor."

"You know, I think I'll ask Jaime to be my best man. We hit it off from day one at work and I like him and his sense of humor." They got all excited then talking about the wedding and making plans. They decided they didn't need to wait a year for the big day since this was a second wedding for the both of them, and settled on October when the maple leaves would be falling and coloring the world beautiful.

"Dad will perform the ceremony of course, but who will walk me down the aisle and give me away? I know it's a second wedding and all and doesn't need all the fanfare of the first, but I still want someone to walk me down the aisle."

"Got a favorite uncle?"

"Yes, Uncle Roger, Dad's brother! He walked me down the aisle at my wedding to Joe. I wonder if he'd be willing to do it a second time?"

"I imagine he will." They continued to talk about their hopes and dreams and agreed they would adopt children. Maddie decided she'd like six children. Rick made a face but held his peace. Finally, as they ran out of things to talk about and their eyelids began drooping, Rick kissed her goodnight, though he really wanted to stay and "celebrate" their engagement. But he knew Maddie would want to wait until their wedding night so he honored that and left.

The following days were full of interruptions by coworkers wanting to know their wedding plans and where they were going on their honeymoon. The honeymoon was the one thing they hadn't discussed yet, but Maddie would make sure she brought it up this evening. Rick talked to Jaime and asked him to be his best man, to which Jaime slapped him on the back, grinned broadly, and agreed. Maddie made arrangements to have lunch with Joan and asked her to be her matron of honor. Joan couldn't say yes fast enough.

The next time Roni, Neal and Melora came in, Maddie asked Roni to be her other matron-of-honor. Roni hugged her and squealed with delight.

Despite all the hullabaloo around their wedding, work still had to get done at the agency. But Maddie now had a bounce in her step as she made home visits to see her foster kids and their parents. Her testimonies in court were done with more precision. She felt like a new woman with a whole new lease on life. The emotional rollercoaster she'd been on since Joe had shown up last November, the horrific beating she'd taken and nearly died from, the hospitalization where the doctors brought her back to life, and then having to tell all the gory details of his attack at the trial had smoothed out, evaporated, especially once Rick had confronted her and wiped out all thoughts of pawning him off on another woman. She sighed with satisfaction. She no longer hurt physically and emotionally. She felt on top of the world. As for spiritually, she couldn't stop thanking God enough for the many blessings He'd bestowed on her: namely, providing her with supportive parents, friends like Joan and Janie, church and work friends, and the doctors and nurses at the hospital. But mostly she thanked God for Rick. He was the blessing she most cherished right now, him and his overwhelming, powerful love for her.

Driving home that evening, she felt healed and ready for the rest of her life. Even if she couldn't bear children, she'd be able to hold her adopted babies and love them from the moment they arrived in her home until the day she died.

Life was good again.

CHAPTER 16

Dangerous Cases

ON A BEAUTIFUL MORNING early in May, Maddie was off to visit a new couple whose children had just recently been removed because of the father's drug use. Maddie's step was light as she hummed to herself on the way up to the door. She'd read the report about the family situation. The father, Peter Brooks, a one-time pro-football player, now retired due to drugs, lived with his wife, Sarah, and two children, Reggie, 5, and Bobby, 3. He was high at the time he hurt his son, and stories abounded in the case file about his belligerence and meanness when high. He had taken out his anger on Reggie this time. His wife was a heavy drinker and was too wasted that afternoon to protect anyone, so both children were removed for their safety. Both parents were court-ordered to attend rehab and parenting classes.

Maddie rang their doorbell. This was her first visit and she wasn't exactly sure what to expect. A tall, muscular black man opened the door.

"Yeah? What do you want?" He wore a sneer on his face and looked Maddie up and down, making her uncomfortable.

"Mr. Brooks? I'm Madison Roper from Child Protective Services. I'm your new caseworker. I called your wife about an hour ago and made an appointment to see the both of you. I'd like to come in and talk with you and your wife if I may."

Brooks stared at her a moment before standing back and letting her in. "Sarah's not here," he said, "but come in anyway."

Maddie noticed his pupils were pinpoints and suspected he was high on something. She felt uncomfortable entering the house without his wife present, but she did, hoping his wife would return quickly.

"Have a seat," he said as he lit a cigarette. Maddie sat on the edge of one of the worn armchairs, tense and alert.

"You say your wife will be home soon?"

"Yeah. In a couple of minutes."

"Good, because I need to talk to the both of you about what happens next and what you need to do to get your children back."

"Look, I just lost my cool, okay? I swatted Reggie harder than I meant to. It was no big deal."

"The report said he had a bloody nose and a black eye, Mr. Brooks. That is considered child abuse."

"I just lost my cool for a moment!" he yelled. Then he deliberately flexed his muscles so she could see how strong and threatening he was.. Maddie fought to stay calm. He was another Joe Skeeter! God help me, she prayed.

"Mr. Brooks, I'm not here to antagonize you," she said soothingly. "I'm here to help you get your children back.

"Like hell you are! You're just like all the rest of them out there, trying to destroy me!"

Maddie stood up in alarm. She needed to get out of the house, away from this man. Suddenly, he pulled out a drawer of an end table near him and brought out a gun, cocking it, and pointed it directly at her. She gasped, her hand flying to her chest.

"Please, Mr. Brooks! Put that away. I'm not here to cause you any trouble! Let me just leave, okay? I won't bother you any longer!" She started edging toward the door, her eyes never leaving the gun pointing at her, which followed her as she skirted by him. Just as she reached for the door handle, the door flew open and Sarah arrived home. Seeing the gun, she immediately got between Maddie and her husband, the bag of groceries in her hand forgotten.

"Peter! Put that damn gun away before you hurt someone!" He stared at his wife defiantly, the gun now aimed at his wife's face. "Peter!" she exclaimed. With a sneer, he slowly lowered the gun to his side and uncocked it.

"She's from Child Protective Services, about the kids," he said. "I don't trust her."

"CPS," said Sarah facing Maddie. "Hi, I'm Sarah Brooks. We spoke on the phone this morning. Please stay. Pete's going to put the gun away right now, aren't you?" Fixing a steady gaze on her husband, she waited while he put it back in the drawer and walked out of the room. Both women sighed with relief.

"I'm so sorry about that," said Sarah, guiding Maddie into the kitchen. "Let's have a cup of coffee and talk. I want to get my kids back."

Maddie let Sarah talk about all the things she was going to do to get control of her drinking and get Pete off drugs so they could get their children back. Maddie listened but she had a feeling that Sarah was just babbling, trying to get Maddie's mind off of Pete pointing his gun at her. Maddie explained to Sarah about the permanency plan the three of them would develop based on the judge's orders, and Sarah nodded her head vigorously that she agreed and would comply.

"What about Pete?" as Maddie. "Will he cooperate, too?"

"Oh, yes! He wants the children back, too."

"Okay, then." Maddie rose, then added, "The next meeting will be at CPS offices. I will not come to this house again and have a gun pointed at me."

"I understand. Thank you for everything, Maddie!" She continued smiling brightly until Maddie was out the door.

Maddie got in her car, a delayed reaction to the fear she felt at the gun pointed at her setting in. Shivering and hands shaking, she returned to CPS. She would tell Janie right away about Brooks threatening her with a gun. She was still shaking when she arrived at CPS and headed straight to Janie's office to relate the whole story. Janie sat with a deep frown on her forehead as she listened. She promptly call the Police Department to inform them and to file an official report. Officer Montgomery came to the office and interviewed Maddie to get the full story.

"You will always have one of my men with you whenever you see Brooks," he told her, "even if the meeting is here at CPS." Maddie's heart sank. This was déjà vu all over again, making her think of Joe. Rick, unfortunately, was out most of the day and she didn't get to talk to him about Brooks until that evening. He was livid.

"I had no idea there could be so much danger in a simple home visit," he said.

"There usually isn't but, obviously, it can and does happen. I'm grateful his wife came home when she did before anything bad happened. I have a bad feeling about the case. The wife, Sarah, promised she'd quit drinking and he'd stop doing drugs. She made it sound simple, like it could happen with a snap of the finger. But I know different."

She and Rick commiserated for a while longer before calling it a night.

The next day, the office was abuzz about Brooks and the gun he'd held on Maddie. During the lunch break, everyone had a story to tell of some harrowing experience they'd endured also.

"When I was the civilian Point of Contact for the Spouse and Child Abuse Team in the Army, I had a woman come after me with a butcher knife," said Molly Watkins, a short pudgy woman adored by everyone. "The lady was about to drop her two-month old baby out of her apartment window," she explained. "The children down below encouraged her, saying they'd catch her, treating it like it was a game. But, fortunately, a neighbor called me and I rushed over there before she let go of the baby. As soon she saw me, she pulled the baby back in and when I got to her apartment, she thrust it at me. I told her I had to remove the baby, which was only about six or eight weeks of age, and her two-year old for their own safety. I figured the woman had post-partum depression. She cried when I told her but she agreed.

"However, as I headed for the door with the children, she suddenly changed her mind and went and grabbed a butcher knife. I slammed the door shut in her face and rushed down to my car and raced to the clinic where the director of the team had his office. After I explained the situation, he immediately called the MPs and two tall, burly guys came over to protect me. The mother got to the clinic and was wandering all over looking for me, knife still in her hand. She was apprehended by the MPs when she reached the room where I was cowering and arrested and jailed her. I learned that her husband had been out in the field for over a month and she wasn't able to handle the children on her own. At any rate, I placed the children in a foster home and then went over to the jail to visit with her. She was sitting on the floor of her cell, crying her heart out, and reached out her arms to me pleading to get her babies back. So I sat on the floor and held her hands and we talked. I got medical attention for her for the depression and they brought her husband home from the field to see how to handle the situation."

"Did she get her children back eventually?" asked one of the group.

"Yeah. It had a happy ending. She was basically sleep-deprived and at her wits end at the time of the incident, but she got her act together once her husband returned home. His sister, a nineteen year old, flew over to Germany to live with them and help out with the children. But it sure was scary being chased by a wild woman with a big knife!"

"I had an incident with a five-month baby who died at the hands of its parents. There was no violence toward me by the parents," said Deloris Caldwell. "The young man was Mexican-American and had lived in the States for several years but returned home to Mexico and married a sixteen-year old Mexico girl who was rather simply-minded. They had a baby girl while in Mexico. Three years later, the father brought them over to the States because his wife was pregnant again. She had a little baby boy whom they named Elvis. At the time, they were living in squalor and Jose had no job, so the children were going hungry and crying a lot. Plus Jose and Maria had terrible fights. At any rate, a neighbor made a report to CPS one day and little Elvis, three-months old at the time, was removed and placed in foster care due to malnutrition and neglect. Jose was ordered by the judge to find a job and a decent apartment to live in.

"Two months later, the judge ordered Elvis returned to the parents with me making daily home visits to check up on them and provide services if they needed any. I made daily visits for about ten days. Then they started not being home when I got there, or pretending not to be, I was never sure. This went on for a few days. Then a call came in that there had been a huge fight. The neighbors heard screaming and crashing sounds and yelling. I hurried over there to find an ambulance pulling away from the apartment and Jose standing in the doorway, glaring and angry. I asked him what happened and he said someone mistakenly called the ambulance but it wasn't needed. Then he slammed the door in my face. I called the office to have someone join me outside of their apartment and I waited to see what happened next. Jaime joined me and as we watched, another ambulance arrived and Maria let them in. We watched in horror as the EMTs wheeled a gurney to the ambulance with a small covered body on it. There were no sirens as they left for the hospital.

"We went over and knocked on the door. Maria answered, only opening the door a crack, but I could see bruises on her face and a split lip. She whispered that Elvis was 'muerte,' which means dead. When she went to close the door, I asked if we could come in. We found the apartment in shambles. Lamps and mirrors were broken, shards of glass were everywhere, the furniture was trashed—it was a real mess. I tried to talk with Maria but she only cried. I tried to talk with their three-year old daughter, Angelica, who always talked a blue-streak whenever I visited, but she wouldn't say a word. We left.

"A couple of hours later a detective called me and asked me to come down to the morgue to identify Elvis' body. It was the first time I'd ever been in a morgue. That poor baby! Dead at five months! The detective told me that the electricity had been turned off and it had been cold in the apartment, so the parents put Elvis on the radiator, wrapped in a blanket, to keep him warm. His body literally dried up until he was dead. I had nightmares for weeks after that! The big fight Jose and Maria had was over calling the ambulance. Maria called twice. Jose refused them entrance the first time but Maria insisted on letting them in the second time. Their daughter, Angelica, never spoke a word since that traumatic event. Almost two years later, she's still mute. And do you want to know the kicker? Jose and Maria went ahead and had another child, a son, and they named him Elvis, too!"

Everyone was silent a moment. Then Jaime spoke. "I haven't had anything like your stories happen to me," he said, "but I did have a wife go after her husband in the car while he ran zig-zag in the street trying to avoid her. He couldn't get away from her, though. She got close enough to hit him and run him over. He ended up with a broken leg, a concussion, and multiple contusions. She was arrested and put in the slammer, but he didn't want to press charges, said he deserved it, and meekly returned home."

A few chuckles lightened the heavy mood of the break room.

Then Monica spoke up. "I had a burned baby case," she said. "The father was giving his year-old daughter a bath in the sink. He deliberately made the water scalding hot and then stuck the baby's feet and legs in that water. He was mad because she was fussing so much. That poor child had third degree burns. I hated that stupid jerk of a father! He did get some jail time for injury to a child, but it wasn't long enough or harsh enough as far as I was concerned."

"How did you work with him feeling that way?" asked Jaime quietly, watching her.

"I didn't want to. I had nothing but contempt for the man. As far as I was concerned, he didn't deserve to ever get his baby back. But Janie made me keep the case and draw up a permanency plan to reunite the family once they'd completed all the judge's orders."

"Where was the mother when this happened?"

"The mother was out shopping at the time and when she heard about what he did, she planned to leave him and run home to Mama. Once the baby was out of the hospital, she was placed with the mother's parents while the couple both got some counseling and decided whether to stay together or not."

"Was the child scarred for life?"

"Yes, but at least she's young enough she won't remember how her feet and legs got that way."

"Can you stand one more sad story?" asked Alice Comings. "My case was about a five-year old named Davey who was left in the family car while his mother went shopping in the mall. It was a hot day in August and the windows were all closed tight. That poor little boy passed out from the heat. Another shopper returning to her car next to Davey's got worried when she saw him slumped over in his car seat. She tapped repeatedly on the window, trying to rouse him. When she couldn't, she called 9-1-1. The boy's mother came out of the mall while the police were there jimmying the door to get him out. He was rushed to the hospital with oxygen and IV fluid."

"Tell me he pulled through," said Rupert Winslow.

"He did and was placed in foster care while mom served her sentence for reckless endangerment of a child."

"My story's probably not as difficult as the rest of yours," chimed in Lois McNeal. "My mother wasn't being a mean mother, she really didn't understand the importance of her daughter's medical condition. Whenever the little girl ate cheese or dairy products, it caused permanent damage to her brain, but the mother let her eat whatever she wanted and the little girl happened to love cheese. Each time she went in to be tested, however, her condition had deteriorated.

"Stupid mother!" commented Monica.

"No, not really stupid. She really didn't get it. Her daughter's deterioration was very gradual and she couldn't see the damage being done so she had a hard time taking it seriously."

Murmurs and head-shakes followed these accounts of scary and sad situations. Most cases didn't provide such drama. Most parents just plodded along obeying, or not obeying, the court orders and eventually, usually after many repeat hearings to spur the parents along, the children would be returned. There were success stories, like the Ordmans, which was even written up in the local newspaper. There were also failures where parental rights were terminated and the children who were young and desirable enough put up for adoption. If not adoptable, they remained wards of the state until they aged out. Rupert, Rick, and three other workers handled those cases, teaching them life skills like how to dress when applying for a job, how to open a checking account, basic shopping and cooking skills, and the like. They did a lot of things with these teenaged foster kids, trying to boost their morale and self-confidence along the way. Several of their kids made it into adulthood successfully but, of course, some also failed.

"Well, I guess it's time to get back to work," commented someone and others reluctantly agreed, finishing their drinks and throwing their trash out.

In her office, Maddie thought about all the unexpected surprises of CPS cases. Being threatened by a gun or a butcher knife was rare, thank goodness. Mostly the workers met resistance on the part of the parents who really didn't want to change their behavior or their lifestyle. Passive-aggressive behavior was the norm. Sometimes parents simply abandoned their kjids and refused to parent them any longer. But most parents eventually knuckled down and followed the court orders and got their children back.

Maddie tried to concentrate on her notes for a court hearing she had that afternoon but her mind flipped back to the Brooks and their hearing next week. She'd have to meet with them beforehand to draw up a permanency plan to present to the judge, but they'd for sure meet here at CPS, with a police officer present. She didn't relish putting herself in any more danger.

That evening, Rick came over to her apartment and she shared some of the stories she'd heard in the breakroom.

"How do you stay professional in situations like those?" he asked. "So far, I haven't encounter anything like that."

"Keep your cool as much as possible, though I'm not sure I did very well with Peter Brooks. If you are threatened but you're allowed to leave, by all means leave as quickly and safely as possible. If you're not allowed to leave, use all the verbal and social work skills you've learned to keep yourself safe. I've never heard of a CPS worker getting killed in the line of duty, if that helps."

"There's always a first time."

"Rick!!"

"Okay," he laughed. "Just joking. Hey. Let's not talk about CPS and danger anymore, okay? I can think of more fun things to talk about, can't you? Like what's going to happen next October, besides the colorful autumn leaves falling, like where we're going to go for our honeymoon, like finding a neat house to buy and moving into it."

"Where are we going to go on our honeymoon?" she asked.

"I was thinking of Aspen or Estes Park or even Mt. Princeton Hot Springs Resort."

"Ooh, a hot springs sounds nice. Will it be open in October?"

"I'll have to research it and find out. But some place like one of those. I might be able to get in some mountain climbing, which I haven't done since November. If I can climb a mountain, I'll know I've regained all my strength back."

"And what will I do while you climb mountains?"

"Learn to ski? Spend the day in the hot springs? Go to the spa? Swim? Learn to kayak? Go shopping?"

"Are you trying to get rid of me already?" she teased.

"No!" Maddie was taken back by his tone of voice.

"I'm sorry," she quickly apologized. "I was just teasing."

"Are you going to have a problem with me going off on a mountain climbing adventure from time to time?" he asked seriously.

"No, Rick, I'm not. Forgive me for my reaction."

There was a moment of strained silence, then Maddie took Rick's hand and raised it to her mouth to kiss it. "I love you, Rick. I was just being a brat."

"Nah," he said with a sigh, "not a brat. Concerned about spending time together on our honeymoon, not apart, that's all. I promise I will only leave you alone for one day, okay?"

"Okay. I can handle that."

Rick nuzzled her nose, then kissed her lips, then drew her close and held her, then. . .

All thoughts of the misunderstanding or other potential problems on their honeymoon vanished as they kissed and reassured each other of their love and devotion.

CHAPTER 17

Marriage and Job Security

It was Monday, five days before her wedding, and Maddie was becoming more and more excited. Her plan was to work through Thursday, then begin her leave so she'd have time to take care of any last minute wedding details on Friday and enjoy the rehearsal and dinner to follow. She planned to have her cases as tidied up as possible for the workers who would cover them while she was gone, plus Janie had promised her no new cases this week.

So, she was incredibly surprised to arrive at the office to find a new case sitting on her desk and a note from Janie telling her to come and get briefed on it when she got in. Annoyed, but trying not to show it, she picked up the file and marched to Janie's office to hear the reason why.

"I'm so sorry to dump this on you at the last minute," Janie apologized. "The case was Monica's, but she and Betsy, the teenager, did not hit it off at all. Betsy Powers is a precocious fifteen year-old who was impregnated by her stepfather, Eugene Hawkins, while stationed overseas. The family arrived here yesterday and were moved into a trailer temporarily. Betsy's baby, Nikki, one-month old, will be placed with the Wheatons by tomorrow, the foster parents who had taken in Susie Q—I mean Melora—several months ago.

"Monica went out this morning to meet with the Hawkins' family and found the parents had taken off during the night for parts unknown, leaving Betsy all alone. Betsy told Monica she wanted to stay there and live by herself and, according to Monica, threw a royal tantrum when Monica told her in no uncertain terms that that was not going to happen, that she would be placed in foster care also. Betsy apparently argued with her, using colorful language, and Monica got so angry she dragged Betsy back here to CPS with her and dumped her in my office. Maddie, you were the only one I could think of to take over Betsy's case."

"But I'll only have a few days with her before I leave."

"I know, dear. I know. But from what I've observed about Betsy in the past half-hour is that she is cute, a huge flirt, brags that she initiated the affair with her stepfather, and desperately needs a friend. Rick is good, and of course Rupert is too, and they both work with teenagers, but they're men and Betsy would wrap them around her little finger so fast they wouldn't know what hit them. I think you would be the best choice as her caseworker. Please take the case, Maddie."

"She sounds like a real spitfire."

"She definitely is! Cute as a button, weighs about 95 lbs., high energy, and very intelligent, very sharp. You'll find her quite fascinating." Janie stood. "Shall we go meet her?" Maddie nodded mutely and stood up too.

A moment later, she met Betsy, who struck her as a whirlwind of energy, standing barely five feet tall, with a pixie haircut that framed her delicate face, and flashing blue eyes. Betsy sized Maddie up, calculating already how to get around this new caseworker. Maddie smiled and reached out her hand to shake Betsy's.

"Hi, I'm Maddie Roper. Let's go into my office and visit a while." She liked Betsy on the spot, sensing her underlying need for love and acceptance. She was convinced Betsy's hunger for attention drove her behavior. Betsy followed Maddie back to her office, looking all around, noticing the male workers and flirting openly with them, until Maddie closed the door to her office and got Betsy's full attention.

"Are you going to be like that Monica?" she asked Maddie.

"No, I'm going to be like me." A small grin appeared on Betsy's face.

"Good, because Monica pissed me off."

"Was it because she insisted on placing you in a foster home? Because I plan to do the same thing, so I guess you can get ready to be pissed at me, too."

Betsy stood still, studying Maddie. "Why? I'm fifteen and I've already proved I'm a woman—I've had a baby."

"Any teenager who menstruates can have a baby; that's not what qualifies them to be considered an adult. To convince a judge you can live on your own you'd have to prove you can work and support yourself, afford an apartment, and have a high school education or a G.E.D. Having babies is not one of the criteria."

"I'll say one thing," said Betsy. "You're definitely not like Monica. She was so damn arbitrary! You at least come across as reasonable."

"Drop the swearing, Betsy. That's also not a requirement for the judge to consider you an adult. Now, tell me, when was the last time you attended school?"

"Last year, I dropped out when the other kids were more interested in me and my big stomach than in the teachers and the teachers got upset."

"Did they ask you to leave?"

"Yeah, but I wanted to anyway. School was boring. I was having more fun screwing Gene than listening to the teachers drone on and on."

"I'm sorry to hear that, Betsy, because we need to get you back in school so you can graduate and get your diploma. First, though, I need to get you to the shelter while I find a foster home for you."

"And Nikki?"

"If there's a home that will take a teenager and a baby, I'll certainly look into it. I noticed you have a suitcase with you, so let's get you over to the shelter for now so you can see your baby."

To Maddie's surprise, Betsy complied without further argument. At the shelter, Betsy sought out Nikki and hugged her. She and the staff got Betsy settled and Maddie headed back to CPS to contact the foster care agency for a home for the two of them. The agency got back to her later in the day to inform her there were none available, at least not at this time. Groaning, Maddie put off going over to tell Betsy the bad news until tomorrow.

When she got to the shelter the next morning, she met with Betsy and Nikki in a meeting room. As kindly as possible, Maddie broke the disappointing news. Anger flashed in Betsy's eyes and she sat up rigidly.

"I want my baby with me!" she snapped at Maddie. "You have no right to separate us!"

"It's not my choice," Maddie answered softly. "But we only have a couple of homes that take teenagers and babies together and they're full right now. Usually, foster parents only takes babies, or young children, or teens, but not a combination." Before Betsy could explode again, Maddie continued. "We'll keep searching, Betsy, but for the time being you and Nikki will go to separate homes. You'll be able to see her daily and care for her, but you won't be able to spend the night together."

Betsy was livid. All at once, she stood up and, without warning, threw Nikki across the room to Maddie, whose heart nearly stopped as she reached up immediately to catch the flying baby. She was scared to death she wouldn't be able to. Nikki let out a scream as she sailed through the air, and, by the grace of God and God alone, Maddie barely caught the baby and hauled her tightly to her chest, her heart beating as wildly as the baby's. Maddie stared open-mouthed at Betsy who was fuming and crying and flushed with rage.

Maddie held Nikki close, cooing to her and gently rocking her, but her eyes never left Betsy's.

"You just lost your chance to be placed together," she told her. "That was reckless endangerment of a child, Betsy! If charges were pressed, you would go to prison."

Betsy sat down, her fury dissipating. She covered her face and cried. "I'm sorry, Maddie! I'm sorry!" Maddie let her cry, willing her own anger and astonishment to subside. In a way, her heart broke for Betsy, who just wanted to love someone and be loved in return. But right now, Maddie knew that her first job was to find a good foster home for Nikki and a separate one for Betsy. Getting up to return the baby to one of aids at the shelter, she told them what happened and asked them to keep Betsy and Nikki apart. Then she went back in to say goodbye to Betsy and left. A foster home for Betsy was found that afternoon and both children were ensconced in their new homes by the end of the day. Maddie went home that night with quite a story to tell Rick.

Unsurprisingly, the next morning, Maddie got a call from Betsy to complain that she didn't like her foster parents, Norm and Irene Springer. She'd already tried to flirt with Norm, but he let her know in no uncertain terms that he wasn't interested. Irene, in Betsy's mind, was too strict and already pushing her to get back in school. She demanded a different foster home. Maddie shook her head and told her no.

"Sorry, Betsy. The Springers are the only home available at present." Betsy ranted and carried on but finally realized she was not going to change Maddie's mind. Maddie waited for the next tirade, but none came.

Then, more quietly, Betsy asked, "Would it be alright if I got a job and went to night school for my G.E.D.?"

"What kind of job could you get? You're only fifteen."

"Dancing."

Carefully, Maddie asked, "What kind of dancing? Ballroom?"

Betsy giggled. "No, in a gentlemen's nightclub."

"You're kidding!"

"No. I've done it before, in Germany. I used to sneak out of the house at night and a couple of other girls and I would go and dance. It was fun! I made lots of money." She was grinning into the phone, imagining the look on Maddie's face.

"Absolutely not!" stated Maddie emphatically. Betsy laughed with delight. "No!" Maddie repeated. "Let's talk about getting your G.E.D. instead."

"Okay! I'll work on it because I want to get emancipated by June."

"What's in June?"

"My birthday. I'll be sixteen then and the judge should be able to grant me my freedom."

"I'll look into a Pell Grant for you. Now," she said, pausing a second for emphasis, "let's talk about what happened yesterday at the shelter. I gather you have an explosive temper, especially when you don't get your way."

"I shouldn't have done that to you. I told you I was sorry."

"Yes, you did, but it's Nikki I'm concerned about."

"You caught her. Anyway, she's too young to ever remember it."

"Regardless, it proves you're not mature enough to be emancipated, Betsy." Betsy's good mood evaporated.

"Does the judge have to know?" she whined.

"Absolutely. I'll explain the circumstances to him, but he's not going to rush to give you emancipation after he hears about it. He may order parenting classes, or anger management. You'll have to jump through many hoops before you even get visitation rights to Nikki."

Betsy listened, sobering. "I just erupt sometimes," she said.

"I understand, but that's something you need to get control of."

"Okay."

After she hung up, Maddie sat and thought for a while. She liked Betsy and wanted her to succeed, to get through the obvious lack of love and nurturing in her life, maybe through therapy, get her G.E.D., and find a decent job. Maybe by then she could get Nikki back, too.

The rest of Thursday was quiet at work and Maddie sighed with relief. She wanted all her cases to stay calm from today until she got back from her honeymoon. However, as it got on for 4:00, she got a phone call from Irene Springer, Betsy's foster mom, telling her Betsy had run away. There'd been an argument and Betsy had stormed out of the house and hadn't returned yet. The police had been notified but hadn't located her.

"Has she made any friends she might have gone to, or maybe over to see Nikki?"

"No friends that we know of, and we checked with Nikki's foster mom. She's not there."

"Okay, Irene. Thanks for the heads-up."

Maddie sank back in her chair, sighing. Betsy was definitely going to be a handful, but she still liked the girl, liked her attempt at making the most out of her life without having been given much direction. What was Doreen Hawkins, Betsy's mother, thinking of? Surely she knew about her husband's philandering? And to side with him when they got to the States and desert her own daughter! No wonder Betsy had so many problems! The one thing Betsy had learned was that she was cute and sexually desirable, so she was capitalizing on what she considered her best traits. But, didn't she realize how smart she was also? Certainly smarter than a lot of fifteen year-olds, education-wise, street-wise, and getting her needs met one way or another.

On her way home that evening, she did her best to put Betsy out of her mind, while praying the whole time for the police to find her and return her safely to the foster home. When Maddie reached her apartment door, she stopped, offered up one last prayer for Betsy, then pushed all thoughts about her out of her mind. Rick would be over tonight and she only wanted to think about him and their future. Of course, she'd tell him the latest on Betsy. In fact, they had devised a plan to deal with their pent up emotions from their cases each day by taking turns venting to each other in the evening and getting everything off their chests so they could relax and enjoy the rest of the time together.

The rehearsal dinner on Friday night went fine and Maddie reveled in it. Her friends had already thrown a wedding shower for her a month earlier and lavished her and Rick with so many gifts for their new home, which they had just purchased. After the dinner, Rick was whisked off for his bachelor party and Maddie went home with her folks for the rest of the evening. She was almost too keyed up to sleep that night, but somehow pulled it off.

Saturday morning arrived bright and sunny, with a nip in the air. It was a perfect fall day for which she thanked God and blessed Him.

At the church getting dressed for the wedding, Joan fussed over her and made sure she had something old, something new, something borrowed, something blue. They heard the music begin to play in the sanctuary and knew the ushers were seating the parents and the attendees. Her Uncle Roger appeared at the door.

"Are you ready for your big moment?" he asked with a broad smile. He was a handsome man with the same ruddy complexion as her father but taller and a little more distinguished looking. Uncle Roger, and his late wife Ellen, were her godparents.

She loved them dearly and had been enormously sad when Ellen contracted cancer and died rather quickly. Maddie was still in college at the time. She went over and hugged her uncle and he kissed her on the cheek.

"I'm ready," she replied. He escorted her to the narthex to watch Joan and Roni be escorted down the aisle to the front of the sanctuary and then patiently waited for the organ to play Purcell's Trumpet Voluntary. Smiling radiantly, Maddie was ready when the organist began to play it and let her uncle escort her to the front, to the man of her dreams, to a future filled with children and lots and lots of love. A niggling thought about Betsy and her other cases penetrated her bliss for a moment, but she resolutely pushed it away. She'd deal with all of them when she returned to work, but not today, not now.

Today was her day!

www.ingramcontent.com/pod-product-compliance
Lightning Source LLC
Chambersburg PA
CBHW031841090426
42741CB00005B/316
* 9 7 8 1 6 3 3 5 7 3 5 8 1 *